RESTORING THE BROKEN FOUNDATIONS

DR. WILLIE JOUBERT

Restoring the Broken Foundations
Copyright © 2020 by Dr. Willie Joubert

All rights reserved. No part of this publication may be reproduced, distributed, or transmitted in any form or by any means, including photocopying, recording, or other electronic or mechanical methods, without the prior written permission of the author, except in the case of brief quotations embodied in critical reviews and certain other non-commercial uses permitted by copyright law.

All Biblical references from the NIV Study Bible Copyright @ The Zondervan Corporation

Tellwell Talent
www.tellwell.ca

ISBN
978-0-2288-3747-3 (Hardcover)
978-0-2288-3746-6 (Paperback)
978-0-2288-3748-0 (Ebook)

ACKNOWLEDGEMENTS

I want to express my sincere appreciation to my wife, Eda, who dared to walk with me as we pursued a vision that took us way beyond our comfort zones. You have indeed encouraged and stretched me and I thank God for that.

A special word of thanks to Jerry and Wilma Vanderveen: You have been such an encouragement and we appreciate your support. I also need to acknowledge the input from Jerry that is the basis of the chapter entitled "Criticism and Rebellion".

I also want to acknowledge Martin and Kim and those who meet at our house as well as the churches that meet at Jerry and Wilma's house and at Roger and Ginette's house. You have truly blessed us and become a living example of the emerging network.

DEDICATION

*T*his book is dedicated to those who dare to dream big dreams and who will not hesitate to pay the price needed to restore the broken foundations of the church.

Table of Contents

ACKNOWLEDGEMENTS iii
DEDICATION v
PREFACE 1
INTRODUCTION 7
THE OLD CANNOT CONTAIN THE NEW 15
THE NEW TESTAMENT MODEL 18
THE INSTITUTIONAL CHURCH 21
RESTORATION OF THE CHURCH 23
FIVEFOLD MINISTRY AND THE
FOUNDATIONS OF THE CHURCH 27
THE HOLY SPIRIT AND THE FIVEFOLD
OFFICES 34
BUILDING A FIVEFOLD CHURCH 42
OBSERVATIONS REGARDING THE CHURCH .. 48
THE CHURCH'S GREATEST UNTAPPED
RESOURCE 52
UNDERSTANDING BIBLICAL LEADERSHIP 63
CHURCH LEADERSHIP THROUGH THE
CENTURIES 73
TOUCH NOT THE LORD'S ANOINTED 77

COVERING 88
CRITICISM AND REBELLION 98
FOUNDATIONS OF COVENANT
RELATIONSHIPS.. 103
EPILOGUE... 124
ABOUT THE AUTHOR 129

PREFACE

*O*n January 24, 1994 the Lord spoke to me in a remarkable way about His body, the church. The Spirit led me to read and study Isaiah 49-58 and as I did, revelation began to flow like never before. At the time I was the minister at West Flamboro Presbyterian Church in Ontario, Canada. In the weeks to follow this continued and I became fascinated with what I found. One of the main themes in these chapters is restoration: restoration of the land; restoration of God's people; restoration of the towns and cities; restoration of the temple. In the original context this referred to the restoration and rebuilding of all that was lost during the exile when the Babylonian forces of Nebuchadnezzar devastated the Kingdom of Judah. However, as I listened to the Spirit, I knew this was a prophetic picture pointing to the restoration of the church.

In a very real way, the vision of the restoration of the church that was birthed in me at the time, set me on a journey to pursue this vision. Without going into details, I will briefly share some of the journey with you. In time I was led to study the other passages of Scripture before and after the chapters, which first caught my attention. Eventually the focus included Isaiah 40-66 and other related passages in Scripture. During the next few years God also challenged and directed Eda and myself and we were moved out of the traditional comfort zone of our church and tradition. In a few short years, we worked in a variety of settings ranging from traditional mainline to independent charismatic churches. We were involved in pastoring a traditional church to bringing restoration to a troubled and divided church to working in non-traditional church planting. We met with both success and failure. After those transitional years we were led to establish 'Breakthrough Prayer Ministries'. In the midst of these transitions we moved from being "clergy" to sitting in the pew. This meant that we were forced to experience and view the ministry from a very different angle. In a very real sense, we discovered the captivity of many of God's anointed; a captivity that came through the structure of the church and its leadership.

During these transitional years, as we spent time in prayer (which ultimately led to the birthing of Breakthrough Prayer Ministries) many intercessors came to us. Without exception they were hurt and broken, through spiritual abuse by the leaders. We were privileged to see broken lives restored and captives set free. However, this also forced us to look at the church structures that lead to these hurts.

To this day, we do not know how some of these broken people found us, but they did. As we ministered to them, we also noted that they were for the most part humble people, strong in their faith and people who moved powerfully in the Spirit. It became clear to us that the insecurity of leaders led them to be controlling and thus they hurt many. These leaders struggled to release those who were more able to minister in some areas than the leaders themselves.

In the midst of these personal experiences, the vision of the restoration of the church kept coming back and it led me to continue to pursue this. One of the key verses that spoke to me in a powerful way was Isaiah 49:8-9a:

> *"This is what the Lord says: 'In time of my favor I will answer you, and in the day of salvation I will help you; I will keep you and make you to be a covenant for the people, to restore the land and to reassign its desolate inheritance, to say to the captives, 'Come out!' and to those in darkness, 'Be free!'"*

This was one of many words that personally spoke to me and we were led to the Scriptures again and again until I was led to the very foundations. As we did, the old truths were revealed (actually they are very obvious!) and the early church's history came to life for us. With that there was a growing yearning to see the church restored and the broken foundations re-laid.

As I said, much of this has been very personal. I kept returning to the Scriptures that came to life for me on January 24, 1994 and Isaiah 49:1-2 burned in my spirit:

> *"Before I was born the Lord called me;*
>
> *From my birth he has made mention of my name.*
>
> *He made my mouth like a sharpened sword; In the shadow of his hand he hid me;*
>
> *He made me into a polished arrow and concealed me in his quiver."*

Finally, when we thought all the work was in vain and it would never happen, God released us to share the message. In a short time, we have witnessed that the ruins can indeed be restored, the foundations re-laid and the desolate inheritances recovered. This little booklet contains the key lessons we learned and the blueprint we found to re-lay the foundations. This booklet will challenge all whose comfort zone is the church that meets in a building to worship once a week and to do the program. It will particularly challenge those who have a vested interest in the current church structure, particularly those in leadership. However, it is not written for them, but for the many who are wandering like sheep without a shepherd. It is intended to help open a door:

> *"to say to the captives, 'Come out!' and to those in darkness, 'Be free!'*
>
> *They will feed beside the roads and find pasture on every barren hill.*
>
> *They will neither hunger, nor thirst, nor will the desert heat or sun beat upon them.*

He who has compassion on them will guide them and lead them beside streams of water.

I will turn all my mountains into roads and my highways will be raised up.

See they will come from afa......"

Shout for joy, O heavens; Rejoice, o earth;

Burst into song, O mountains!

For the Lord comforts his people and will have compassion on his afflicted ones."

Isaiah 49:9-13

INTRODUCTION

The church of Jesus is in transition and the molds of tradition are cracking open. Some are moving into new paradigms – even kicking and screaming, but moving nonetheless. Others are holding on for dear life while some are content to die with "the church" as they know it.

This little book is not intended to convince anyone that change is coming or needed. It is simply a reflection of what is happening and a basic study of what Jesus intended the church to be. It is also my belief that what is actually happening is a restoration of the church to become what Jesus intended it to have been from the beginning.

When we talk about the church there are some key pictures in Scripture:

1. The church is a building and Jesus the cornerstone:

   ## 1 Corinthians 3:10-15

   By the grace God has given me, I laid a foundation as an expert builder, and someone else is building on it. But each one should be careful how he builds.

   For no one can lay any foundation other than the one already laid, which is Jesus Christ. If any man builds on this foundation using gold, silver, costly stones, wood, hay or straw, his work will be shown for what it is, because the Day will bring it to light. It will be revealed with fire, and the fire will test the quality of each man's work. If what he has built survives, he will receive his reward. If it is burned up, he will suffer loss; he himself will be saved, but only as one escaping through the flames.

   ## Ephesians 2:19-22

   Consequently, you are no longer foreigners and aliens, but fellow citizens with God's people and members of God's household, built on the foundation of the apostles and prophets, with Christ Jesus himself as the chief cornerstone. In him the whole building is joined together and rises to become a holy temple in the Lord. And in him you too are being built together to become a dwelling in which God lives by his Spirit.

2. The church is a body and Jesus is the head:

   ## 1 Corinthians 12:12-31

   The body is a unit, though it is made up of many parts; and though all its parts are many, they form one body. So it is with Christ. For we were all baptized by one Spirit into one body-whether

Jews or Greeks, slave or free-and we were all given the one Spirit to drink.

Now the body is not made up of one part but of many. If the foot should say, "Because I am not a hand, I do not belong to the body," it would not for that reason cease to be part of the body. And if the ear should say, "Because I am not an eye, I do not belong to the body," it would not for that reason cease to be part of the body. If the whole body were an eye, where would the sense of hearing be? If the whole body were an ear, where would the sense of smell be? But in fact God has arranged the parts in the body, every one of them, just as he wanted them to be. If they were all one part, where would the body be? As it is, there are many parts, but one body.

The eye cannot say to the hand, "I don't need you!" And the head cannot say to the feet, "I don't need you!" On the contrary, those parts of the body that seem to be weaker are indispensable, and the parts that we think are less honorable we treat with special honor. And the parts that are unpresentable are treated with special modesty, while our presentable parts need no special treatment. But God has combined the members of the body and has given greater honor to the parts that lacked it, so that there should be no division in the body, but that its parts should have equal concern for each other. If one part suffers, every part suffers with it; if one part is honored, every part rejoices with it.

Now you are the body of Christ, and each one of you is a part of it. And in the church God has appointed first of all apostles, second prophets, third teachers, then workers of miracles, also those having gifts of healing, those able to help others, those with gifts of administration, and those speaking in different kinds of tongues. Are all apostles? Are all prophets? Are all teachers? Do all work miracles? Do all have gifts of healing? Do all speak in tongues? Do all interpret? But eagerly desire the greater gifts. And now I will show you the most excellent way.

Ephesians 1:19-23

His incomparably great power for us who believe is like the working of his mighty strength, which he exerted in Christ when he raised him from the dead and seated him at his right hand in the heavenly realms, far above all rule and authority, power and dominion, and every title that can be given, not only in the present age but also in the one to come. And God placed all things under his feet and appointed him to be head over everything for the church, which is his body, the fullness of him who fills everything in every way.

3. Jesus is the vine and we are the branches bearing fruit:

John 15:1-17:

I am the true vine, and my Father is the gardener. He cuts off every branch in me that bears no fruit, while every branch that does bear fruit, he prunes so that it will be even more fruitful. You are already clean because of the word I have spoken to you. Remain in me, and I will remain in you. No branch can bear fruit by itself; it must remain in the vine. Neither can you bear fruit unless you remain in me.

I am the vine; you are the branches. If a man remains in me and I in him, he will bear much fruit; apart from me you can do nothing. If anyone does not remain in me, he is like a branch that is thrown away and withers; such branches are picked up, thrown into the fire and burned. If you remain in me and my words remain in you, ask whatever you wish, and it will be given you. This is to my Father's glory, that you bear much fruit, showing yourselves to be my disciples.

As the Father has loved me, so have I loved you. Now remain in my love. If you obey my commands, you will remain in my love, just as I have obeyed my Father's commands and remain in his love. I have told you this so that my joy may be in you and that your joy may be complete. My command is this: Love each other as I have loved you. Greater love has no one than this, that he lay down his life for his friends. You are my friends if you do what I command. I no longer call you servants, because a servant does not know his master's business. Instead, I have called you friends, for everything that I learned from my Father I have made known to you. You did not choose me, but I chose you and appointed you to go and bear fruit-fruit that will last. Then the Father will give you whatever you ask in my name. This is my command: Love each other.

The important issue to note in all of these pictures is that Jesus is the center in each one. To understand what the church is to be, we need to know Jesus and when we look at Him, we need to know that He was controversial! He did not fit the mold!

The one thing about Jesus was that He was one who had authority, e.g. in Matthew 7:28-29 we read:

> *When Jesus had finished saying these things, the crowds were amazed at his teaching, because he taught as one who had authority, and not as their teachers of the law.*

It amazed many for they knew He had no formal training, but everything He did illustrated His authority – over demons, disease and in teaching, preaching, etc.

Jesus' major problem was with the religious system of His day, which was controlled by leaders who used their position to exercise power and control over many, and who greatly benefited from the system economically, politically and socially. In a word, they controlled people through the rules and regulations they had set up and through the control of the sacrificial system tied to the building called the temple.

Jesus clashed with them as He set ordinary people free and released them to minister:

Luke 9:1-6:

When Jesus had called the Twelve together, he gave them power and authority to drive out all demons and to cure diseases, and he sent them out to preach the kingdom of God and to heal the sick. He told them: "Take nothing for the journey-no staff, no bag, no bread, no money, no extra tunic. Whatever house you enter, stay there until you leave that town. If people do not welcome you, shake the dust off your feet when you leave their town, as a testimony against them." So they set out and went from village to village, preaching the gospel and healing people everywhere.

Luke 10:1-24:

After this the Lord appointed seventy-two others and sent them two by two ahead of him to every town and place where he was about to go. He told them, "The harvest is plentiful, but the workers are few. Ask the Lord of the harvest, therefore, to send out workers into his harvest field. Go! I am sending you out like lambs among wolves. Do not take a purse or bag or sandals; and do not greet anyone on the road. When you enter a house, first say, `Peace to this house.' If a man of peace is there, your peace will rest on him; if not, it will return to you. Stay in that house, eating and drinking whatever they give you, for the worker deserves his wages. Do not move around from house to house.

When you enter a town and are welcomed, eat what is set before you. Heal the sick who are there and tell them, `The kingdom of God is near you.' But when you enter a town and are not welcomed, go into its streets and say, `Even the dust of your town that sticks to our feet we wipe off against you. Yet be sure of this: The kingdom of God is near.' I tell you, it will be more bearable on that day for Sodom than for that town.

Woe to you, Korazin! Woe to you, Bethsaida! For if the miracles that were performed in you had been performed in Tyre and Sidon, they would have repented long ago, sitting in sackcloth and ashes. But it will be more bearable for Tyre and Sidon at the judgment than for you. And you, Capernaum, will you be lifted up to the skies? No, you will go down to the depths.

He who listens to you listens to me; he who rejects you rejects me; but he who rejects me rejects him who sent me."

The seventy-two returned with joy and said, "Lord, even the demons submit to us in your name."

He replied, "I saw Satan fall like lightning from heaven. I have given you authority to trample on snakes and scorpions and to overcome all the power of the enemy; nothing will harm you. However, do not rejoice that the spirits submit to you, but rejoice that your names are written in heaven."

At that time Jesus, full of joy through the Holy Spirit, said, "I praise you, Father, Lord of heaven and earth, because you have hidden these things from the wise and learned, and revealed them to little children. Yes, Father, for this was your good pleasure.

All things have been committed to me by my Father. No one knows who the Son is except the Father, and no one knows who the Father is except the Son and those to whom the Son chooses to reveal him."

Then he turned to his disciples and said privately, "Blessed are the eyes that see what you see. For I tell you that many prophets and kings wanted to see what you see but did not see it, and to hear what you hear but did not hear it."

The main issue was that Jesus broke with the concept of a religious system controlled by a few and taught that everyone could walk in a personal relationship with God the Father and He illustrated that through His lifestyle. **As we look at the church, this issue will come up again and again, for the church as most of us know it is little different** in this respect from the system Jesus challenged. In fact, one of the key pictures Jesus used is one of new wineskins needed for the new wine and we will turn our attention to this for a moment.

THE OLD CANNOT CONTAIN THE NEW

Luke 5:33-39:

"They said to him, 'John's disciples often fast and pray, and so do the disciples of the Pharisees, but yours go on eating and drinking.' Jesus answered, 'Can you make the guests of the bridegroom fast while he is with them? But the time will come when the bridegroom will be taken from them; in those days they will fast.' He told them this parable: 'No one tears a patch from a new garment and sows it on an old one. If he does, he will have torn the new garment, and the patch from the new will not match the old. No one pours new wine into old wineskins. If he does the new wine will burst the skins, the wine will run out and the wineskins will be ruined. No, new wine must be poured into new wineskins. And no one after drinking old wine wants the new, for he says, 'The old is better.'"

Throughout His ministry Jesus was questioned about his lifestyle and teaching – e.g. the passage above. After answering the immediate question regarding fasting, Jesus focused on the key issue and that was if the old religious system could be changed to receive His message of freedom through a relationship with God. Speaking about the birthing of the church, Jesus plainly stated that the old system would not be able to contain the new Kingdom mindset – like an old wineskin the new wine will burst it and it will not work. However, He also stated that many would not move with the new, preferring the old saying it is better! Those set in their ways would be too inflexible and the system would not receive the new concepts.

This actually happened! The church that was birthed on the day of Pentecost (Acts 2) started with 120 in the upper room praying and being filled with the Spirit. They then moved into the street where the church was born and 3000 new believers were added that day. This was prophetic because the church cannot be contained in a building! They tried to hang in with the old for a while, meeting in the temple. Later, Paul for example, would begin in the synagogues, but every time they met resistance and persecution and were forced out.

The key issue that caused major problems was the fact that they walked in a faith based on a relationship with Jesus and therefore they walked in authority, as we read for example in Acts 4:5-14:

> *The next day the rulers, elders and teachers of the law met in Jerusalem. Annas the high priest was there, and so were Caiaphas, John, Alexander and the other men of the high priest's family. They had Peter and John brought before them*

and began to question them: "By what power or what name did you do this?"

Then Peter, filled with the Holy Spirit, said to them: "Rulers and elders of the people! If we are being called to account today for an act of kindness shown to a cripple and are asked how he was healed, then know this, you and all the people of Israel: It is by the name of Jesus Christ of Nazareth, whom you crucified but whom God raised from the dead, that this man stands before you healed. He is "`the stone you builders rejected, which has become the capstone.' Salvation is found in no one else, for there is no other name under heaven given to men by which we must be saved."

When they saw the courage of Peter and John and realized that they were unschooled, ordinary men, they were astonished and they took note that these men had been with Jesus. But since they could see the man who had been healed standing there with them, there was nothing they could say.

They spoke with boldness and did miracles. **The key to recognize is that a relationship cannot be contained by rules and regulations – but religion can! Every relationship is unique – e.g. friendships and marriage!** The church that was birthed on the day of Pentecost when the new wine was released could not fit into the old wineskin of Judaism. The personal relationship with a living risen Savior could not be fitted into the old system with its rules and regulations. It needed a totally new wineskin, called the church.

THE NEW TESTAMENT MODEL

*T*he early Christians did not need a special building, as most meetings took place in homes (Acts 2:46 and 18:7 and Romans 16:5). When they needed or wished to gather in a group too large for a house, they used existing buildings, e.g. the Temple in Jerusalem (Acts 2:46), the local synagogue (Acts 14:1) or if that was denied, a rented building (Acts 19:9) or open air (Acts 16:13). They had no program for which a specially designed building was essential.

Meetings were held in local homes and businesses. The meetings were simple and included a time to worship, prayer, fellowship with food and the Lord's supper, teaching and ministry which included miracles, prophesy, etc. (Acts 2:42-47, 4:23-31, 13:1-3, etc.) All participated and gifts were encouraged and released. There were no special programs tailored to meet needs of groups like children, youth, singles, etc. As all were included and gifts recognized and released, with true fellowship in small groups, needs were met within the body through body ministry.

Local leaders led home churches. Broader oversight was exercised by apostles and others (Acts 8:14-17 and 11:22-24), recognized and accepted by the house groups as leaders, often because they planted these churches (1 Corinthians 9:2) or on recommendation from a recognized leader (Ephesians 6:21-22 and Colossians 4:7-9). Financial matters were easy to handle and the home church directed the finances as they deemed best and necessary, often with great generosity (2 Corinthians 8:1-15). The overhead was low, as they met in the homes and shared meals together. With leadership being local with no professional clergy and no shared building, tithes and offerings could support the need of the poor and special projects (Acts 4:32-37, 6:1-6, 11:27-30) as well as blessing leaders (Philippians 4:10-20). Leadership was recognized, developed and strengthened through relationship, working together (Acts 13:1-4 and 16:6). Ministry was entrusted to the members and the leaders were to equip them to do this work (Ephesians 4:11-13). The equipping was done by recognizing and imparting gifts, as well as mentoring, e.g. Timothy who was mentored by Paul, travelling and working alongside him (Acts 11ff.) and then was commissioned by Paul with laying on of hands (2 Timothy 1:6). Those being mentored were gradually released into ministry and often became mentors themselves, thus building the body. Leaders supported themselves or were supported through gifts by the members (1 Corinthians 9:14 and Philippians 4:10-20).

The church birthed on the day of Pentecost and set free from the confines of religious controls, continued to grow. It thrived amidst persecution and literally transformed the societies wherever believers went. Then in the midst of this the very success a door opened that would tie the church up for centuries. It is to this that we need to turn our focus, before we look at the restoration of the church.

THE INSTITUTIONAL CHURCH

*I*n the 4th century the Emperor Constantine became a believer. With his conversion the persecution of Christians came to an end and the church became an official part of the Roman Empire. Gradually the leaders began to introduce the political structure of this Empire into the church. Leadership developed into a hierarchy and it led yet again to a system of manipulation and control with professionals in power. Using programs and rituals and special buildings ordinary people became spectators. Some changes occurred through the Reformation (another wineskin split), but the structure of the church remained as we've known it in recent times, basically involving the following:

1. *Professional clergy in leadership, trained in an approved college or seminary.*
2. *A Board of elected or appointed leaders to oversee the church program.*
3. *Programs to meet the various perceived needs, e.g. educational needs, property, management, finances, etc.*
4. *A set time(s) for worship with the clergy in prominent leadership.*
5. *The church building where most of the meetings and programs are held.*

Within this structure there is variety, e.g. the style of music, the form of worship, the chosen way of leadership and management, etc. However, the above elements are part and parcel of the church in the Western world and the church battles mostly center on particular ways of dealing with one or more of the above. If you try e.g. to introduce contemporary worship in a traditional setting, you will face a battle. Or try to change the set time of worship or the order of worship and see what happens. The spirit of control often joins with a religious spirit to bring division into the church through any of the elements described above. In fact, a simple thing like introducing contemporary music can cause the structure to crack and the wineskin to burst! So, guess what will happen if we seriously consider getting back to the New Testament model of the church?

RESTORATION OF THE CHURCH

We are at a time and a place in history where God is restoring the church to the original model displayed in the New Testament. I firmly believe that God has said: "Enough is enough!" I believe that He is restoring the church as He intended it to have been in the first place. The old wineskins are going to pop wide open as He releases the new wine!

A key passage is Ephesians 4:7-16:

> *"But to each one of us grace has been given as Christ apportioned it. This is why it says:*
>
> *'When he ascended on high, he led captives in his train and gave gifts to men.' (What does 'he ascended' mean except that he also descended to the lower earthly regions? He who descended is the very one who ascended higher than all the heavens, in order to fill all the universe. It was he who gave*

> *some to be apostles, some to be prophets, some to be evangelists, and some to be pastors and teachers, to prepare God's people for works of service, so that the body of Christ may be built up until we all reach unity in the faith and in the knowledge of the Son of God and become mature, attaining to the whole measure of the fullness of Christ. Then we will no longer be infants, tossed back and forth by the waves, and blown here and there by every word of teaching and by the cunning and craftiness of men in their deceitful scheming. Instead, speaking the truth in love, we will in all things grow up in him who is the head, that is, Christ. From him the whole body, joined and held together by every supporting ligament, grows and builds itself up in love as each part does its work."*

Jesus when He ascended divided the office that He had into five offices (each of which He is the key model): Apostles, Prophets, Evangelists, Pastors and Teachers. He appointed people in these offices as gifts to the church so that they would equip and release every member of the church to the work of ministry. We will look at this in detail later, but the main thing to note is that **the ultimate goal of the church is to have every member fully released in ministry so that the whole church will work in unity as a team.**

Another important passage is 1 Peter 2:4-10:

> *"As you come to him, the living stone – rejected by men but chosen by God and precious to him – you also, like living stones, are being built into a spiritual house to be a holy priesthood, offering spiritual sacrifices acceptable to God through Jesus Christ. For in Scripture it says:*

> *'See, I lay a stone in Zion, a chosen and precious cornerstone, and the one who trusts in him will never be put to shame.'*
>
> *Now to you who believe, this stone is precious. But to those who do not believe, 'the stone the builders rejected has become the capstone,' and 'a stone that causes men to stumble and a rock that makes them fall.' They stumble because they disobey the message – which is also what they were destined for. But you are a chosen people, a royal priesthood, a holy nation, a people belonging to God, that you may declare the praises of him who called you out of darkness into his wonderful light. Once you were not a people, but now you are the people of God. Once you had not received mercy, but now you have received mercy."*

Again, without going into the detail at this point, this passage plainly states, that every believer is to act as a priest in ministry with divine royal authority. Every member of the church has been called to ministry and should be in ministry.

This is the time for body ministry – where every one of us is in ministry wherever we go! It is time to "go back to the future!"

The new wine that is being poured by God is nothing else but the wine that was being poured out 2000 years ago before the church turned it off! It was not intended to ever stop. God never intended the church to stop with body ministry. He did not set up the structures we have in most churches. He did not call some to be professionals to do ministry in a set building and maintain programs. God never ordained the wineskins we have!

This wine may be new to us, but it is the vintage old wine! It has been aged and is the best wine and those who taste this wine will not want the wine used in most churches today! The current structure of the church will not be able to handle this wine and it will break if we try to pour this wine into it. God's Kingdom does not need a building or a program. It is based on relationship and accountability that comes through relationships. It gives authority to each believer to walk in power over evil, led by the Spirit.

The only way this will become a full reality is through a network of interdependent home churches committed to walk in unity through relationship, just as we read in the New Testament. The Apostles and Prophets of our day will lay foundations and help to birth these churches and to raise up leaders and encourage and release people. Their main task is to come alongside the members and to encourage them to become all that God intended them to be and do! Leadership in this model is exercised by serving and in this service, authority flows out of relationship.

God is raising apostolic leaders to set up such networks and to encourage the birthing of home churches. True body ministry where every member will function in his/her call cannot work in large settings. It has to take place in small groups. From time to time house churches will unite to have a celebration and worship. At other times they will gather with key speakers, e.g. apostles or prophets in a rented facility. The restoration of the New Testament Church is at hand and with that we need to look at leadership and foundational issues.

FIVEFOLD MINISTRY AND THE FOUNDATIONS OF THE CHURCH

Introduction

*A*s we have seen, Jesus said the old wineskins would not be able to handle the new wine (Luke 5:37-39). To use another picture, the foundations need to be laid anew. The major problem with the church goes right to the foundations. It is foundational when we consider that Paul said that the foundations are to be laid by Apostles and Prophets with Jesus as cornerstone (Ephesians 2:20). Now, the fact is that most churches do not believe that these offices are valid today! It is no wonder we have so many problems in the church! If we do not accept these offices, then who laid the foundations of our churches?

Before we look at this in more detail, we need to again look at Ephesians 4:11-16, which is the divine blueprint for the church:

> *"It was he who gave some to be apostles, some to be prophets, some to be evangelists, and some to be pastors and teachers, to prepare God's people for works of service, so that the body of Christ may be built up until we all reach unity in the faith and in the knowledge of the Son of God and become mature, attaining to the whole measure of the fullness of Christ. Then we will no longer be infants, tossed back and forth by the waves, and blown here and there by every word of teaching and by the cunning and craftiness of men in their deceitful scheming. Instead, speaking the truth in love, we will in all things grow up in him who is the head, that is, Christ. From him the whole body, joined and held together by every supporting ligament, grows and builds itself up in love as each part does its work."*

It says that Jesus when He ascended took the five offices He held and divided them and gave as gifts to the church these five offices: Apostles, Prophets, Evangelists, Pastors and Teachers. These offices were to work in unity in building the church by equipping and releasing the members into their call and ministry. **The idea was that the whole church would be doing the work of ministry as Jesus did. In fact, Jesus expected that we would do even more! Read with me John 14:12-17:**

> *"<u>I tell you the truth, anyone who has faith in me will do what I have been doing. He will do even greater things than these,</u> because I am going to the Father. And I will do whatever you*

ask in my name, so that the Son may bring glory to the Father. You may ask me for anything in my name, and I will do it. If you love me, you will obey what I command. And I will ask the Father and he will give you another Counselor to be with you forever – the Spirit of truth. The world cannot accept him, because it neither sees him nor knows him. But you know him, for he lives with you and will be in you."

Let us put these words in perspective. This was Jesus talking on the eve of His last day with his disciples. He knew that He would die the next day. Now, if you and I know this is the last time we will talk with our closest friends – the last hour together – would we talk about baseball or hockey or would we try to make our words count? The answer is obvious. Jesus was trying to convey the key issues regarding His life and ministry to His followers. In very clear words He said that <u>anyone who has faith in Him, would do what He did and even greater things than that!</u> The whole purpose of the church is to do the ministry of Jesus. Jesus expected that and if we follow His blueprint for the church, it will happen. The key to open the door is to have those called to these five offices doing their work to equip and release the members to do their ministry.

Jesus is the Model of the fivefold ministry offices:

- He is the chief apostle as we read in Hebrews 3:1

    Therefore, holy brothers, who share in the heavenly calling, <u>fix your thoughts on Jesus, the apostle</u> and high priest whom we confess.

The word "Apostle" is a Greek word that means someone sent on a mission with authority to do the work. Jesus is the key apostle, for He was sent by the Father, for we read John 3:16, *"For God so loved the world that he gave his one and only Son, that whoever believes in him shall not perish but have eternal life."* He came on a mission with the goal to finish the work.

John 4:34 reads: *"Jesus said, 'My food is to do the will of him who sent me and to finish his work.'"*

Not only was Jesus sent He also sent His disciples, as we read in John 20:21:

"Again Jesus said, 'As the Father sent me, so I send you.'"

In Matthew 28:18-20 we read how He sent the disciples with the words: *"All authority in heaven and on earth is given to me. Therefore go and make disciples of all nations, baptizing them in the name of the Father and of the Son and of the Holy Spirit, and teaching them to obey everything I have commanded you. And surely I am with you always, to the very end of the age."*

- He was a prophet.

When Jesus raised a young man from the dead, we read in Luke 7:16 *"They were all filled with awe and praised God. 'A great prophet has appeared among us,' they said."* Jesus also prophetically spoke regarding the destruction of Jerusalem and the signs of the end times (Matthew 24:1-34). After His resurrection

He appeared to many, including the two men on the way to the town of Emmaus. He joined their conversation and asked what they were talking about. They replied (Luke 24:19), "*We talk about Jesus of Nazareth. He was a prophet, powerful in word and in deed before God and all the people.*"

- He was the key evangelist.

He had a heart for the lost and reached out to them. Because of this He was often criticized, for He tended to reach out to those rejected by society and by the religious establishment. One such occasion was recorded in Luke 19:1-10. It is the story of Zacchaeus, the rich rejected tax collector. Jesus spotted him in a tree where he climbed to get a glimpse of Jesus. When Jesus saw him, He called and visited him at home and enjoyed a meal there. The story ends with Jesus saying: *"Today salvation has come to this house, because this man, too, is a son of Abraham. For the Son of Man came to seek and save what was lost."* Jesus is the key evangelist.

- He was the good Shepherd and the word shepherd is the same word we use for pastor.

He said this about Himself (John 10:11 and 14-15): "*I am the good shepherd. The good shepherd lays down his life for his sheep. I am the good shepherd. I know my sheep and my sheep know me – just as the Father knows me and I know the Father – and I lay down my life for my sheep.*" That was exactly what He did on a lonely hill outside Jerusalem where He laid down His life for His sheep. After that, as the good Shepherd He appointed others to shepherd the flock, like Peter whom He called again at the Sea of Galilee and three times charged to take care of the flock and feed the lambs (John 21:15-19). His example as pastor was such that this Peter wrote the following to the elders in 1 Peter 5:1-4: *"To the elders among you, I appeal as a fellow elder, a witness of Christ's sufferings and one who will also share in the glory to be revealed: Be shepherds of God's flock that is under your care, serving as overseers – not because you must, but because you are willing as God wants you to be; not greedy for money, but eager to serve; not lording it over those entrusted to you, but being examples to the flock. And when the Chief Shepherd appears, you will receive the crown of glory that will never fade away."*

- He was the teacher that taught with authority so that people were amazed.

This first happened when He taught what we know as "the sermon on the mount" and we read Matthew 7:28-29: *"When Jesus had finished saying these things, the crowds were amazed at his teaching, because he taught with authority, and not as their teachers of the law."*

Nicodemus, the Pharisee who paid Him a secret visit said to Him: *"<u>Rabbi, we know you are a teacher who has come from God</u>. For no one could perform the miraculous signs you are doing if God were not with him."* (John 3:2).

Jesus taught with authority and in word and in deed, knowing that He was sent as teacher. Just before He was arrested and crucified, He washed the feet of the disciples and when He finished, He said to them (John 13:13-17):

"<u>You call me 'Teacher' and 'Lord,' and rightly so, for that is what I am</u>. Now that I, your Lord and Teacher, have washed your feet, you should also wash one another's feet. I have set you an example that you should do what I have done for you. I tell you the truth, no servant is greater than his master, nor is a messenger greater than the one who sent him. Now that you know these things, you will be blessed if you do them."

However, Jesus was not the only model of the fivefold offices. Let us consider the work of the Holy Spirit in this regard.

THE HOLY SPIRIT AND THE FIVEFOLD OFFICES

Introduction:

*J*ust before Jesus ascended into heaven, He told His disciples to wait in prayer for the Holy Spirit, recorded in Acts 1:4-8. *"On one occasion, while he was eating with them, he gave them this command: 'Do not leave Jerusalem, but wait for the gift my Father promised, which you have heard me speak about. For John baptized with water, but in a few days, you will be baptized with the Holy Spirit.' So, when they met together, they asked him, 'Lord, are you at this time going to restore the kingdom to Israel?' He said to them: 'It is not for you to know the times or dates the Father has set by his own authority. But you will receive power when the Holy Spirit comes on you; and you will be my witnesses in Jerusalem, in Judea and Samaria, and to the ends of the earth.'"* The

Spirit would equip and empower them to do the work of ministry.

Ten days later on the day of Pentecost the Holy Spirit came and filled those gathered in the upper room as we read in Acts 2:

> *When the day of Pentecost came, they were all together in one place. Suddenly a sound like the blowing of a violent wind came from heaven and filled the whole house where they were sitting. They saw what seemed to be tongues of fire that separated and came to rest on each of them. All of them were filled with the Holy Spirit and began to speak in other tongues as the Spirit enabled them.*

That is the same Spirit that is available to help us and the power they received is the same power we have available to us! In fact, read Ephesians 1:17-21: *"I keep asking that the God of our Lord Jesus Christ, the glorious Father, may give you the Spirit of wisdom and revelation, so that you may know him better. I pray also that the eyes of your heart may be enlightened in order that you may know the hope to which he has called you, the riches of his glorious inheritance in the saints, and <u>his incomparably great power for us who believe. That power is like the working of his mighty strength which he exerted in Christ when he raised him from the dead and seated him at his right hand in the heavenly realms, far above all rule and authority, dominion and power, and every title that can be given, not only in the present age, but also in the one to come.</u>"* Just keep that in mind as we move on, for we will return to this and tie it in with what follows.

The fivefold ministry of the Holy Spirit:

But the Holy Spirit is also a fivefold Spirit! The Spirit in us is a fivefold Spirit in the same way Jesus ministered in the fivefold ministry. In fact, Jesus ministered only in the power of the fivefold Holy Spirit. Jesus did not minister on this earth as the divine Son of God, but as the Son of man. Philippians 2:6-8 states very clearly that He set aside His divinity while on earth to become fully human. He, the divine Son of God, became a man and lived a fully human life and died as human on the cross and was raised bodily as human.

> *"Jesus Christ, being in very nature God, did not consider equality with God something to be grasped (to hang onto it),*
>
> *but made himself nothing, taking the very nature of a servant and being made in human likeness.*
>
> *And being found in appearance as a man, he humbled himself and became obedient to death – even death on a cross!*
>
> *Therefore God exalted him to the highest place and gave him the name that is above every name, so that at the name of Jesus every knee should bow, in heaven and on earth and under the earth, and every tongue confess that Jesus Christ is Lord, to the glory of God the Father."*

Jesus did not begin His ministry until He was baptized by John and at that moment the Holy Spirit came upon Him to equip Him for the work of ministry and He began His work of ministry on earth. Everything He did flowed from the Holy Spirit, including the fivefold ministry. Let us look at it as we did with Jesus:

- **First the Holy Spirit is an Apostolic Spirit:**

   He was sent by Jesus and by the Father. Let us read John 14:25-26 and 15:26-27:

   > *"'All this I have spoken while still with you. But the counselor, whom the Father will send in my name, will teach you all things and will remind you of everything I have said to you.'*
   >
   > and 'When the counselor comes, whom I will send to you from the Father, the Spirit of truth who goes out from the Father, he will testify about me. And you must also testify, for you have been with me from the beginning.'"*

   The Holy Spirit is also a sending Spirit as we read in Acts 13:1-4:

   > "*In the church at Antioch there were prophets and teachers: Barnabas, Simeon called Niger, Lucius of Cyrene, Manaen (who had been brought up with Herod the tetrarch) and Saul. While they were worshiping the Lord and fasting, the Holy Spirit said: 'Set apart for me Barnabas and Saul for the work to which I have called them.' So, after they had fasted and prayed, they placed their hands on them and sent them off. The two of them, sent on their way by the Holy Spirit, went down to Seleucia and sailed from there to Cyprus.*"

- **The Holy Spirit is a Prophetic Spirit:**

   Peter wrote about their witness regarding Jesus and how that confirmed the word of the prophets and then He added the following in 2 Peter 1:20-21:

> *"Above all, you must understand that no prophesy of Scripture came about by the prophet's own interpretation. For prophecy never had its origin in the will of man, but men spoke from God as they were carried along by the Holy Spirit."* Prophecy is simply put a speaking forth of revelation from the Holy Spirit and He is the author of prophecy.

- **The Holy Spirit is also an Evangelistic Spirit:**

He is evangelistic, because He brings conviction as Jesus said in John 16:8-11:

> *"When the Counselor comes, he will convict the world of guilt in regard to sin and righteousness and judgment: in regard to sin, because men do not believe in me; in regard to righteousness, because I am going to the Father where you can no longer see me; and in regard to judgment, because the prince of this world now stands condemned."*

This role of the Spirit was clearly revealed on the day of Pentecost when Peter spoke and explained to the crowd about the resurrection and that the risen and exalted Christ *"has received from the Father the promised Holy Spirit and has poured out what you now see and hear. Therefore, let all Israel be assured of this: God has made this Jesus, whom you crucified, both Lord and Christ."* (Acts 2:32-36). Then we read in the next verse: *"When the people heard this, they were cut to the heart and said to Peter and the other apostles, 'Brothers, what shall we do?'"* The presence of the Holy Spirit caused the witness of Peter to bring conviction leading to the salvation of 3,000 that day.

- **The Holy Spirit is also a Teaching Spirit:**

In John 14:24-26 Jesus speaking to the disciples said:

> *"He who does not love me will not obey my teaching. These words you hear are not my own; they belong to the Father who sent me. All this I have spoken while still with you. But the Counselor, the Holy Spirit, whom the Father will send in my name, will teach you all things and will remind you of everything I have said to you."*

Later that night He also said the following to them (John 16:12-15):

> *"I have much more to say to you, more than you can now bear. But when he, the Spirit of truth, comes, he will guide you into all truth. He will not speak on his own; he will speak only what he hears, and he will tell you what is yet to come. He will bring glory to me, by taking from what is mine and making it known to you. All that belongs to the Father is mine. That is why I said that the Spirit will take from what is mine and make it known to you."*

- **Finally, the Holy Spirit is also a Pastoral Spirit:**

We read about this in a very interesting passage in the Book of Acts where Paul was on his way to Jerusalem, knowing through the Spirit that he was facing hardships and imprisonment. Meeting with the elders from Ephesus in Miletus, Paul spoke to them and charged them to care for the people in the following words (Acts 20:28-31): *"Keep watch over yourselves and all the flock of which the Holy Spirit has made you overseers. Be shepherds of the church of God, which he bought with his own blood. I know that after I leave, savage wolves will come in among you and will not spare the flock. Even from your own number men will arise and distort the truth in order to draw away disciples after them. Be on guard!"* The very essence of the Spirit is pastoral and this is also why He comes alongside us to help us in our weakness and intercedes for us as Paul wrote in Romans 8:26-27: *"In the same way the Spirit helps us in our weakness. We do not know what we ought to pray for, but the Spirit himself intercedes for us with groans that words cannot express. And he who searches our hearts knows the mind of the Spirit, because the Spirit intercedes for the saints in accordance with the will of God."*

<u>Jesus did His ministry in and through the Holy Spirit. When He ministered in any aspect of the fivefold ministry offices, He was led and empowered by the Holy Spirit who is the fivefold Spirit behind the offices.</u> **This means that in every believer there is a deposit of the fivefold. It does not mean that every believer is an apostle or a prophet – but to a degree we each need to function in the fivefold gifts.** Everyone needs to know that there is a specific call and mission from God for one's life! Every person should be able to speak forth a prophetic word. Every one of us should be able and willing to share the gospel with someone. Every one of us should be able to lead someone in the truth and every one of us should

have a pastoral heart to care for others. Corporately every church should have the fivefold Spirit operating when they meet!

Now, before we move to the practical aspects of the fivefold ministry, let us just consider the corporate anointing and the words of Jesus quoted from John 14:12-17 where Jesus said that we would do even greater things than what He did. Again, when Jesus ministered in person on earth, He did this as a single human through the anointing of the Spirit. <u>Today Jesus is doing His ministry as risen Lord working corporately through the anointing released in the members of His body, the church. Where we come together corporately in His name, He manifests as risen Lord and works in and through us as the anointing of the Spirit is released. There is tremendous power when we come together in the name of Jesus!</u>

BUILDING A FIVEFOLD CHURCH

*H*ow does it work in practical terms? How do we build a church that the wineskin will hold the new wine? It starts with the foundation. Let us read the blue print from 1 Corinthians 3:10-11: *"By the grace God has given me, I laid a foundation as an expert builder, and someone else is building on it. But each one should be careful how he builds! For no one can lay any foundation other than the one already laid, which is Jesus Christ."* Another key passage is Ephesians 2:19-22: *"Consequently, you are no longer foreigners and aliens, but fellow citizens with God's people and members of God's household, built on the foundation of the apostles and prophets, with Christ Jesus himself as the chief cornerstone. In him the whole building is joined together and rises to become a holy temple in the Lord. In him you too are being built together to become a dwelling in which God lives by his Spirit."*

Any building begins with Foundations. The foundation determines the size, shape and strength of the building. **Foundations must be laid by Apostles and Prophets, for this is God's order as Paul wrote in 1 Corinthians 12:27-28:** *"Now you are the body of Christ and each of you is a part of it. And in the church God has appointed first of all apostles, second prophets, third teachers, then workers of miracles, also those having gifts of healing, those able to help others, those with gifts of administration and those speaking in different kinds of tongues."*

Apostles are first in time, rank and order. The anointing of the Apostle is a pioneering anointing. They move with more power and authority than anyone in the church. They need this as they are called to break new ground, move into new territory and begin new works. They work closely with prophets, because prophets are second in rank and they have the ability to see and picture the shape and size of the building. They work as a team to draw up the blueprints through revelation and begin the foundations. Sometimes they are called in to restore broken foundations and re-lay the foundations.

Let us turn to a wonderful prophetic word from the Old Testament to illustrate the fivefold ministry. This passage in Isaiah 51:1-2 was a word to encourage God's people to return from the exile and rebuild the ruins of Jerusalem and the temple after the exile. Many were discouraged and this word was a powerful encouragement to them: *"Listen to me, you who pursue righteousness and who seek the Lord: Look to the rock from which you were cut and the quarry from which you were hewn: Look to Abraham, your father, and to Sarah who gave you birth. When I called him, he was but one and I blessed him and made him many!"*

Let us now tie this picture to the one mentioned by the apostle Peter in 1 Peter 2:4-10: *"As you come to him, the living stone – rejected by men but chosen by God and precious to him – you also, like living stones, are being built into a spiritual house to be a holy priesthood, offering spiritual sacrifices acceptable to God through Jesus Christ. For in Scripture it says:*

> *'See, I lay a stone in Zion, a chosen and precious cornerstone, and the one who trusts in him will never be put to shame.'*
>
> *Now to you who believe, this stone is precious. But to those who do not believe, 'the stone the builders rejected has become the capstone,' and 'a stone that causes men to stumble and a rock that makes them fall.' They stumble because they disobey the message – which is also what they were destined for.*
>
> *But you are a chosen people, a royal priesthood, a holy nation, a people belonging to God, that you may declare the praises of him who called you out of darkness into his wonderful light. Once you were not a people, but now you are the people of God. Once you had not received mercy, but now you have received mercy."*

The Apostle and Prophet draw up the blueprint as they work together and they lay the foundations as a team. Once the foundations are laid with care taken that Jesus is the cornerstone, they begin to build. The evangelist is the one who works in the quarry and cuts the stones and blasts the rock to get the stone out. The anointing of the evangelist is an anointing to find the living stones for the building. However, the evangelist is usually not very good at shaping these stones and putting the finishing touches on each one. The teacher is the one anointed to shape the stones – cutting the rough edges off and preparing them to be built into the wall. The pastor is the one filling in the cracks and nursing the stones so that they will not fall and break. The pastor is anointed to carry the stones, cut and uncut, shaped and rough around the building site.

As this building is being built, these five offices are all vital. They work together supporting one another in amazing ways. The prophet sees the potential of each living stone and works with the teacher to shape it into the form it should be. The prophet also directs the evangelist to potential future quarries to get more stones. The pastor works with the evangelist to pick up the newly blasted stones and move them to the building site. The apostle keeps the overall view in mind, overseeing the team and working with the prophet to finish the building. There is a finishing anointing that comes through the apostolic leadership. Remember that Jesus is the model and in John 4:34 He said about His apostolic mission: *"My food is to do the will of him who sent me and to finish his work."* In fact, just before He went to the cross, we read that He prayed to the Father (John 17:1-4) and said: *"Father, the time has come. Glorify your Son, that your Son may glorify you. For you granted him authority over all people that he might give eternal life to all those you have given him. Now this is eternal life: That they may know you, the only* *true God, and Jesus Christ whom you have sent. I have brought you glory on earth by completing the work you gave me to do."* The last words on His lips when He died (John 19:30) were: ***"It is finished!"***

The Apostolic anointing to lay foundations and finish the work is illustrated in the story of the rebuilding of the temple. The picture painted in Isaiah 51 literally came to pass as the Jews returned from the exile and rebuilt the city and restored the temple. The prophet Zechariah played a major part as he encouraged Zerubbabel, who as apostolic leader was the person who laid the foundations of the temple. In Zechariah 4 there is a vision of the lamp stand with a bowl at the top with 7 lights and 7 channels to the lights and two olive trees, one on each side. Then in Chapter 4:6-10 we read: *So the angel said to me, "This is the word of the Lord to Zerubbabel: 'Not by might nor by power, but by my Spirit,' says the Lord Almighty. 'What are you, O mighty mountain? Before Zerubbabel you will become level ground. Then he will bring out the capstone to shouts of 'God bless it! God bless it!' Then the word of the Lord came to me: 'The hands of Zerubbabel have laid the foundation of this temple; his hands will also complete it.' Then you will know that the Lord Almighty has sent me to you. Who despises the day of small things? Men will rejoice when they see the plumb line in the hand of Zerubbabel."*

In the same way as this rebuilding of the physical temple by Zerubbabel, encouraged and stirred up by the prophetic words of Haggai and Zechariah, began and was completed, so does Jesus build His church through teams of Apostles and Prophets. They lay the foundations and work with the team to finish the work and bring glory to God. Using Jesus as the cornerstone, they lay foundations and applying the plumb line, they build a solid and enduring church. It is not done through power or might – not through human design and ingenuity, but by the Spirit of God.

OBSERVATIONS REGARDING THE CHURCH

*I*n some church circles many talk about this, but few churches practice this. **The fivefold ministry is not about titles, but about fruit.** Jesus spoke about fruit on more than one occasion. In fact, one of the key passages regarding the church is the picture of the vine and the branches in John 15:1-17. Let us look at this picture for a moment: *"I am the true vine and my father is the gardener. He cuts off every branch in me that bears no fruit, while every branch that does bear fruit, he prunes so that it would be even more fruitful. You are already clean because of the word I have spoken to you. Remain in me and I will remain in you. No branch can bear fruit by itself; it must remain in the vine. Neither can you bear fruit unless you remain in me. I am the vine and you are the branches. If a man remains in me and I in him, he will bear much fruit; apart from me you can do nothing.*

If anyone does not remain in me, he is like a branch that is thrown away and withers; such branches are picked up, thrown in the fire and burned. If you remain in me and my words remain in you, ask whatever you wish, and it will be given to you. This is to my Father's glory, that you bear much fruit, showing yourselves to be my disciples."

In a similar way Jesus warned the disciples against false prophets in these words, recorded in Matthew 7:15-20: *"Watch out for the false prophets. They come to you in sheep's clothing, but inwardly they are ferocious wolves. By their fruit you will recognize them. Do people pick grapes from thorn bushes, or figs from thistles? Likewise, every good tree bears good fruit and every bad tree bears bad fruit. A good tree cannot bear bad fruit and a bad tree cannot bear good fruit. Every tree that does not bear good fruit is cut down and thrown into the fire. Thus, by their fruit you will recognize them."*

Let us apply these words to the church. It is not only applicable to individual lives, but also corporately. That is why Jesus, for example, sent the letters to the seven churches in the Book of Revelation, for He expected fruit in these churches. The fivefold ministry should produce fruit. **The fruit of the fivefold ministry are fully functioning churches where these five offices are in operation and where the members are equipped and released in their gifts.** It is not about titles and "apostles" ruling over the people! It is about equipping and releasing people into ministry and about members of the body ministering to one another. If people are sitting in the pew or chair and are not released, it is not the church that Jesus came to establish. The most effective way to do this is to allow people to do ministry. Jesus did not wait to first perfect the disciples – he sent them out and then sat down with them afterwards (Luke 9). Note that He even allowed Judas to do ministry and Peter was not quite perfect and John and James had some problems with envy and were power hungry at the time! <u>It is in the process of doing ministry that members are equipped and that they grow to become more effective</u>.

In each believer are the fivefold Holy Spirit and all His gifts and where He is there is freedom, for 2 Corinthians 3:17 reads: *"Now the Lord is Spirit and where the Spirit of the Lord is, there is freedom."* In everyone who believes, is resident the power and potential that raised Jesus from the dead and seated Him in heaven in the place of authority, for Ephesians 1:19-22 says: *"The power for us who believe is incomparably great! It is like the working of God's mighty strength, which he exerted in Christ when he raised him from the dead and seated him at his right hand in the heavenly realms, far above all rule and authority, power and dominion, and every title that can be given, not only in this present age, but also in the age to come."* **One of the foundational aspects of the task of apostles and prophets is to stir up the gifts and the potential in every believer and to set each one free to be the powerhouse God made that individual to be!** The fruit of a fully functioning fivefold church is seen in how many of the members are equipped and released to do their ministry. It is precisely at this point that the wineskins are beginning to break, for the truth that every believer is called to ministry and should be set free, is causing major stress to the structure of the church in the Western world! There is a huge untapped resource about to be released and the old structures will break under the strain.

THE CHURCH'S GREATEST UNTAPPED RESOURCE

Introduction:

Just prior to his arrest, death and resurrection, Jesus spoke extensively regarding the end times and His return to this earth. Matthew recorded His words to the crowds and to His disciples in chapters 23-25 of his gospel. Included in these final words of Jesus, is a story about the talents. Let us read this story together, for it is a crucial story for us as we approach the time of His return to this earth: Matthew 25:14-30.

"Again, it will be like a man going on a journey, who called his servants and entrusted his property to them. To one he gave five

talents of money, to another two talents and to another one talent, each according to his ability. Then he went on his journey. The man who had received the five talents went at once and put his money to work and gained five more. So also, the one with the two talents gained two more. But the man who had received the one talent went off, dug a hole in the ground and hid his master's money.

After a long time, the master of those servants returned and settled accounts with them. The man who had received the five talents brought the other five. He said: 'Master, you entrusted me with five talents. See, I have gained five more!' His master replied: 'Well done, good and faithful servant! You have been faithful with few things; I will put you in charge of many things. Come and share your master's happiness!' The man with the two talents also came. 'Master,' he said, 'you entrusted me with two talents; see, I have gained two more!' His master replied: 'Well done, good and faithful servant! You have been faithful with a few things; I will put you in charge of many things. Come and share your master's happiness!'

Then the man who had received the one talent came. 'Master,' he said, 'I knew that you are a hard man, harvesting where you have not sown and gathering where you have not scattered seed. So, I was afraid and went out and hid your talent in the ground. See, here is what belongs to you.' His master replied: 'You wicked, lazy servant! So, you knew that I harvest where I have not sown and gather where I have not scattered seed? Well then, you should have put my money on deposit with the bankers, so that when I returned, I would have received it back with interest! Take the talent from him and give it to the one who has the ten talents. For everyone who has will be given more, and he will have an abundance.

Whoever does not have, even what he has will be taken from him. Throw that worthless servant outside, into the darkness, where there will be weeping and gnashing of teeth.'"

Most messages on this parable ignore the larger context and focus on individual members of the church and their gifts. This is not wrong and it certainly addresses one level of meaning, but I want to focus on the larger context. This context began with Jesus' criticism of the religious leaders of His day. In chapter 23:1-14 Jesus sharply criticized them for we read: *"Then Jesus said to the crowds and to his disciples, 'The teachers of the law and the Pharisees sit in Moses' seat. So, you must obey them and do everything they tell you. But do not do what they do, for they do not practice what they preach. They tie up heavy loads and put them on men's shoulders, but they themselves are not willing to lift a finger to move them. Everything they do is done for men to see: They make their phylacteries wide and the tassels on their garments long; they love the place of honor at banquets and the most important seats in the synagogues; the love to be greeted in the marketplaces and have men call them 'Rabbi.'*

'But you are not to be called 'Rabbi,' for you only have one Master and you are all brothers. And do not call anyone on earth 'father', for you have one Father and he is in heaven. Nor are you to be called 'teacher,' for you have one teacher, the Christ. The greatest among you will be your servant. For whoever exalts himself will be humbled and whoever humbles himself will be exalted.'

'Woe to you, teachers of the law and Pharisees, you hypocrites! You shut the kingdom of heaven in men's faces. You yourselves do not enter, nor will you let those enter who are trying to enter.'"

Application in the church:

Let us put these together and apply them to the church leadership structure that we have in most churches today: The greatest untapped resource in the church are the people sitting in the pew and all the gifts being buried in the process! Those who are in leadership are unwilling to open the door of ministry to the believers. The leaders of most churches are literally no different than those in Jesus' day. We see many willing and able workers carrying loads of responsibility to oversee and run ineffective programs year in and year out. These programs are being developed and packaged in the denominational headquarters and sold to the churches to continue the bureaucracy, but the programs do not change lives or touch communities.

The leadership structures in the churches are set up to leave the control of the ministry in the hands of the professionals. Many of the clergy are taught and trained in schools that deny the power and gifts of the Spirit. Like the Pharisees and teachers of the law, they themselves do not enter the Kingdom of heaven that Jesus spoke about, nor do they allow those who try to enter to get in.

The saddest part is that **even many leaders who do believe in the power and the gifts of the Spirit do not release most of the members into ministry**. The only gifts being "released" are those recognized to run the programs and needed to fill the slots. Allow me to illustrate this with two personal examples: I met on a weekly basis with two great brothers in the Lord for months. They were the pastors of a local fellowship. As I observed the lack of release of members in this fellowship, very early on I drew up a list of the key members of the church and asked these brothers individually to list the main spiritual gifts of each member and then in another column to indicate how that person's gifts were being released in the church. They agreed, but it has been years and even though I really insisted that this be done – I am still waiting! They did not do this, for it would have exposed the fact that most gifts were not being released. In another church we went through the "gift tests" and gifts were identified, but that was the extent of the exercise! Weeks of work and hours of the members' time ended in a file somewhere in the church and no members were released into ministry as a result. All that happened was that members knew which gifts they had, but that was all. The list can continue, but the reality is that most churches have most members and gifts buried in the pews!

The way I see it, every church leader is entrusted with the management of the resources given by the Lord. We take tremendous pains to ensure that we account for every penny given to the church and will scrutinize the financial accounts and audit the books in detail, especially since we report to the government as charities. This is not unlike the way the Pharisees did with their tithes. This is good – but **the key resources entrusted to the leadership are the people!**

They are more important than the tithes and offerings! The gifts of God released in His people are far more valuable and it is time to account for the way these are released to serve the Kingdom. To understand this better, we need to look at another picture of the church, and that is the church being the body of Christ in which every part is functioning according to God's design.

Body ministry:

The apostle Paul talked about the church as the body of Christ in a number of key passages: Romans 12, 1 Corinthians 12-14 and Ephesians 1:22-23 and 4:1-16. Let us look at each of these briefly:

> Romans 12:1-8: *"Therefore, I urge you, brothers, in view of God's mercy, to offer your bodies as living sacrifices, holy and pleasing to God – this is your spiritual act of worship. Do not conform any longer to the pattern of this world, but be transformed by the renewing of your mind. Then you will be able to test and approve what God's will is his good, pleasing and perfect will. For by the grace given me I say to each one of you: Do not think of yourselves more highly than you ought, but rather think of yourself with sober judgment, in accordance with the measure of faith God has given you. Just as each of us has one body with many members, and these members do not all have the same function, so in Christ we who are many form one body, and each member belongs to all the others. We have different gifts, according to the grace given us. If a man's gift is prophesying, let him use it in proportion to his faith. If it is serving, let him serve; if it is teaching, let him teach; if it is encouraging, let him encourage; if it is contributing to*

the needs of others, let him give generously; if it is leadership, let him govern diligently; if it is showing mercy, let him do it cheerfully."

The main thrust of the passage is that we commit to give all we have to serve God. This service must lead to use the gifts we individually received from Christ to serve one another. In the following passage (Romans 12:9-21) Paul turns the focus on the attitude needed when serving one another and in practical terms outlines how every act of service needs to flow from a sincere love for the members of the body. The same message is found in 1 Corinthians 12-14, just in an expanded form. Paul began this passage by saying that we must be knowledgeable regarding the gifts of the Spirit and that each gift is unique and functions in a unique way though different people. Then he stresses that every single member of the body is important and should be recognized and released to minister to the others through the gifts given to each one. Central to the release of gifts and the service to one another is love, for without true love our service and gifts mean little, and this is outlined in 1 Corinthians 13 as the most excellent way. In the following chapter Paul again speaks about the gifts, particularly prophecy and speaking in other tongues. In the closing passage regarding the gifts and their release in the body, he gives guidelines for the release in the service of worship including the following (1 Corinthians 14:26): *"What then shall we say, brothers? When you come together, everyone has a hymn, or a word of instruction, a revelation, a tongue or an interpretation. All of these must be done for the strengthening of the church."*

These passages clearly state that the body is made for ministry. Every member is important to the others and called to minister. With this in mind, we now move to Ephesians where the same issues are raised, but this time from the perspective of the church structure of leadership. Jesus is the head of the body and everything else is under his headship. As risen Lord He was raised to the position of power and authority and appointed as head over everything for His body, the church (Ephesians 1:18-23): *"I pray also that the eyes of your heart may be enlightened in order that you may know the hope to which he has called you, the riches of his glorious inheritance in the saints, and his incomparably great power for us who believe. That power is like the working of his mighty strength which he exerted in Christ when he raised him from the dead and seated him at his right hand in the heavenly realms, far above all rule and authority, dominion and power, and every title that can be given, not only in the present age, but also in the one to come."*

This risen Lord, Jesus, when He ascended, took His office and divided it into five offices of leadership. Those called to the fivefold ministry are to equip the members and then release them into the ministry (Ephesians 4:11-16): *"It was he who gave some to be apostles, some to be prophets, some to be evangelists, and some to be pastors and teachers, to prepare God's people for works of service, so that the body of Christ may be built up until we all reach unity in the faith and in the knowledge of the Son of God and become mature, attaining to the whole measure of the fullness of Christ. Then we will no longer be infants, tossed back and forth by the waves, and blown here and there by every word of teaching and by the cunning and craftiness of men in their deceitful scheming. Instead, speaking the truth in love, we will in all things grow up in him who is the head, that is, Christ. From him the whole body, joined and held together by every supporting ligament, grows and builds itself up in love as each part does its work."*

The church is called to body ministry! The measure of the effectiveness in leadership is how many members are equipped **and released**. I want to stress the last two words: **AND RELEASED!** In our churches we have countless programs where we supposedly equip and train people. Churches are forever running courses and studies! **But most members are never released!**

Again, consider the model of Jesus and how He operated: Jesus sent the 12 before they were perfected in their training (Luke 9) – and it even included Judas! Then He sent out 72 others (and their names are not in the Book). These no-names bound demons and caused Satan to fall from heaven! Luke 10:17-18: *"The seventy-two returned with joy and said: 'Lord, even the demons submit to us in your name!' He replied: 'I saw Satan fall like lightning from heaven. I have given you authority to trample on snakes and scorpions and to overcome all the power of the enemy. Nothing will harm you. However, do not rejoice that the spirits submit to you, but rejoice that your names are written in heaven."* **There are countless numbers of no-names called and equipped by the Spirit that are shackled by fearful and insecure leaders and sitting in the pews or wandering from church to church – many very anointed!**

More than that: The very size of our gatherings makes it virtually impossible to practice body ministry! It forces us to have a few ministering and the rest sit in the pews. It is time to move out of the four walls and into the homes, businesses and streets again. Every wall built by human hands will come down. Two of the key walls that are breaking as the wineskin is bursting with the new wine, are the walls between the church and the world and between the clergy and laity.

This is no different than the days Jesus walked this earth. The final straw that caused the religious leaders to plot to kill Him was when He entered the temple and cleansed it. Let us read Matthew 21:12-16: *"Jesus entered the temple area and drove out all who were buying and selling there. He overturned the tables of the moneychangers and the benches of those selling doves. 'It is written' he said to them, 'My house will be called a house of prayer, but you are making it a den of robbers.' The blind and lame came to him at the temple, and he healed them. But when the chief priests and the teachers of the law saw the wonderful things he did and the children shouting in the temple area, 'Hosanna, to the Son of David!' they were indignant. 'Do you hear what these children are saying?' they asked him. 'Yes,' Jesus answered, have you never read, 'From the lips of children and infants you have ordained praise?'"*

Today Jesus is again stepping into the church and He is cleaning it up and setting His people free. It is time for the wonderful things to be returned – for the blind and the lame to be healed and captives set free. It is time for the children to rejoice and silence the enemy! (Psalm

8:2). It is time for God's people to be released into their call and ministry so that the body can be built up and the world reached.

This will only happen if every member is released and body ministry becomes common again. This can only work in small groups and God is moving the church out of the four walls and into the world and homes – and the new wine is being served! The task of the fivefold ministry is to come alongside the members and enable each one to fulfil his or her destiny for the Kingdom. Just as it happened when the church was birthed, so will the current structures break down and shatter and those religious leaders who have a vested interest in the current structures will persecute many who move with the Spirit. But just as the persecution could not stop the move of the Holy Spirit in the days of the Book of Acts, so will the current leadership and controls not stop the move of the Spirit in our day and age. As Jesus said repeatedly to the churches in the Book of Revelation: **"He who has an ear to hear, let him hear what the Spirit says to the churches!"**

With that we need to look at the issues of leadership in the church.

UNDERSTANDING BIBLICAL LEADERSHIP

Introduction:

*T*here are two models of leadership in the Bible. They are both Kingship models, but there is a general failure in the church to distinguish between the two models. As a result, there is much confusion in the church when it comes to leadership structures, yet these are foundational matters for the church.

Model 1:

This model can be illustrated as a pyramid with the leadership on top overseeing and ruling over those underneath. This model is best illustrated by the Kingship in the Old Testament. The King was

anointed to rule! (e.g. 1 Samuel 10:1) The King lived in the Palace with servants (e.g. 2 Samuel 7:1) and had a throne (e.g. 2 Samuel 7:13) and special royal robes (e.g. 1 Kings 22:10)! He rode in a chariot and had an army to protect him (e.g. 1 Kings 22:34). Close to the King – in the ideal context – were Prophets and Priests – **anointed** e.g. King David – Prophet Nathan – Priest Zadok.

The question to be asked is this: How well did this model work?

The answer is that it did not work very well for the following reasons:

- Lack of accountability and silencing of critics. It started with the first king in Israel, Saul and it continued throughout the period of the monarchy. There are numerous examples, e.g. Jezebel's threat to kill Elijah (1 Kings 19:1-2) and the treatment of Jeremiah (e.g. Jeremiah 26:7-11).

- Opens door for spirit of elitism. One of the key phrases used in this context is the quote from David in 1 Samuel 26:9 "Do not touch God's anointed!" We will need to look at this again in detail later, but it is part and parcel of the package.

- When problems arise, the system leads to control often based on fear and it is maintained by violence. There are numerous examples, beginning with Saul and right to the end of the monarchy.

- Leadership often eliminates potential leadership that could pose a threat. Saul's pursuit of David is a classic example and it did not stop there. Solomon consolidated his throne by executing his brother Adonijah with his supporters, including Joab and Abiathar.

However, the key reason why this model did not work well was that it was not God's preferred model from the start! Let us look at 1 Samuel 8:

As Samuel got old, he appointed his sons to be leaders. They were not men of integrity as he was and the people came and said: *"You are old and your sons do not walk in your ways; now appoint a king to lead us, such as all the other nations have."* (1 Samuel 8:5) It is very important to note that the people asked for the model that they saw in other nations – the model of the world.

As the story continues, we read how Samuel was not in agreement and sought God on this. Then we read: 1 Samuel 8:7-9: *"And the LORD told him: 'Listen to all that the people are saying to you: it is not you they have rejected, but they have rejected me as their king. As they have done from the day I brought them up out of Egypt until this day, forsaking me and serving other gods, so they are doing to you. Now listen to them; but warn them solemnly and let them know what the king who will reign over them will do.'"*

Samuel then spelled out the price of the model of leadership they requested. As we read 1 Samuel 8:10-18 we find that this model had a very high price tag and Samuel concluded with a warning: 1 Samuel 8:18: *"When that day comes, you will cry out for relief from the king you have chosen, and the LORD will not answer you in that day."*

However, the people refused to listen to Samuel and said: *"No, we want a king over us. Then we will be like other nations, with a king to go out before us and fight our battles."* (1 Samuel 8:21). <u>Note the fact that they asked for the model of leadership like the other worldly nations and the reason was that they wanted a human person to protect them and fight their battles – even at the high price spelled out by Samuel.</u>

<u>Model 2:</u>

Jesus also had a kingdom model in mind. He spoke extensively about the Kingdom of God or the Kingdom of heaven. However, in terms of leadership Jesus turned the whole model described above upside down, because the Kingdom of God is an upside-down Kingdom.

Let us look at Matthew 20:20-28: *"Then the mother of Zebedee's sons came to Jesus with her sons and, kneeling down, asked a favor of him. 'What is it you want?' he asked. She said, 'Grant that one of these two sons of mine may sit at your right and the other at your left in your kingdom.' 'You don't know what you are asking,' Jesus said to them. 'Can you drink the cup I am going to drink?' 'We can,' they answered. Jesus said to them, 'You will indeed drink from my cup, but to sit at my right or left is not for me to grant. These places belong to those for whom they have been prepared by my Father.' When the ten heard about this, they were indignant with the two brothers. Jesus called them together and said, 'You know that the rulers of the Gentiles lord it over them, and their high officials exercise authority over them. Not so with you. Instead, whoever wants to become great among you must be your servant, and whoever wants to be first must be your slave – just as the Son of Man did not come to be served, but to serve, and to give his life as a ransom for many.'"*

True leadership comes by serving! Jesus not only said this, but He personally illustrated this through His life and mission. It is the way of the cross. Let us read Philippians 2:1-11: *"If you have any encouragement from being united with Christ, if any comfort from his love, if any fellowship with the Spirit, if any tenderness and compassion, then make my joy complete by being like-minded, having the same love, being one in spirit and purpose. Do nothing out of selfish ambition or vain conceit, but in humility consider others better than yourselves. Each of you should look not only to your own interests, but also to the interests of others. Your attitude should be the same as that of Christ Jesus: Who, being in very nature God, did not consider equality with God something to be grasped, but made himself nothing, taking the very nature of a servant, being made in human likeness. And being found in appearance as a man, he humbled himself and became obedient to death – even death on a cross! Therefore God exalted him to the highest place and gave him the name that is above every name, that at the name of Jesus every knee should bow, in heaven and on earth and under the earth, and every tongue confess that Jesus Christ is Lord, to the glory of God the Father."*

This Jesus who became a servant even unto death on a cross is the cornerstone of the church. The key to the foundation of the church laid by apostles and prophets (see 1 Corinthians 4:1 and 9-13) is the servant leadership taught and illustrated by Jesus. There is a personal price to be paid by those called to leadership e.g. the apostle Paul who laid the foundation of the church in Corinth like an expert builder (1 Corinthians 3:10) speaks about this in the very next chapter:

1 Corinthians 4:9-13: *"For it seems to me that God has put us apostles on display at the end of the procession, like men condemned to die in the arena. We have been made a spectacle to the whole universe, to angels as well as to men. We are fools for Christ, but you are so wise in Christ! We are weak, but you are strong! You are honored, we are dishonored! To this very hour we go hungry and thirsty, we are in rags, we are brutally treated, we are homeless. We work hard with our own hands. When we are cursed, we bless; when we are persecuted, we endure it; when we are slandered, we answer kindly. Up to this moment we have become the scum of the earth, the refuse of this world."*

Servant leadership is costly. It is not how many are under you that count, but how many are you lifting and holding up! Servant leadership comes by way of the cross and this message is foolishness to the world:

> 1 Corinthians 1:18-25: *"For the message of the cross is foolishness to those who are perishing, but to us who are being saved it is the power of God. For it is written: 'I will destroy the wisdom of the wise; the intelligence of the intelligent I will frustrate.' Where is the wise man? Where is the scholar? Where is the philosopher of this age? Has not God made*

foolish the wisdom of the world? For since in the wisdom of God the world through its wisdom did not know him, God was pleased through the foolishness of what was preached to save those who believe. Jews demand miraculous signs and Greeks look for wisdom, but we preach Christ crucified: a stumbling block to Jews and foolishness to Gentiles, but to those whom God has called, both Jews and Greeks, Christ the power of God and the wisdom of God. For the foolishness of God is wiser than man's wisdom, and the weakness of God is stronger than man's strength."

Not only does the message of the cross sound foolish to the world, but especially when it is applied to leadership. When you turn the picture of a pyramid upside down it looks unstable! However, the stability does not depend on how broad the base is – it is what is underneath the structure. The first model is built on the sand of humanity and worldly wisdom and the second model is built on the eternal Rock as Peter wrote in 1 Peter 2:4-7a: *"As you come to him, the living Stone – rejected by man but chosen by God and precious to him – you also, like living stones, are being built into a spiritual house to be a holy priesthood, offering spiritual sacrifices acceptable to God through Jesus Christ. For in Scripture it says: 'See, I lay a stone in Zion, a chosen and precious cornerstone, and the one who trusts in him will never be put to shame.'"*

This stone called Jesus was rejected because He did not fit the worldly leadership model. His message of the cross and of servant leadership was rejected and with that they rejected Him too. He did not look like the traditional cornerstone. But to this day those who accept

Him are chosen and precious stones that are being built into a spiritual house to be a holy priesthood. I am indebted to Kim from our house church who shared with me that the stability of this house comes through the shape of our living and eternal cornerstone. It is not a simple upside-down pyramid with apostles and prophets at the bottom. As the building is being built Jesus as cornerstone comes underneath this upside-down pyramid supporting every layer as the living stones are put in place. This church will not be shaken and the gates of hell will not stand against it, as we read in Matthew 16:15-19:

> *"But what about you?" Jesus asked. "Who do you say I am?"*
>
> *Simon Peter answered, "You are the Christ, the Son of the living God."*
>
> *Jesus replied, "Blessed are you, Simon son of Jonah, for this was not revealed to you by man, but by my Father in heaven. And I tell you that you are Peter, and on this rock, I will build my church, and the gates of Hades will not overcome it. I will give you the keys of the kingdom of heaven; whatever you bind on earth will be bound in heaven, and whatever you loose on earth will be loosed in heaven."*

Jesus himself will build his church and it will be perfected to be according to His blueprint and run by servant leaders and nothing else. His model is not the worldly model, but the model of the Kingdom. Apostles and prophets called by and anchored to the eternal Rock, Jesus, lay the foundation with a willingness to shoulder the load. But there is more to this: this upside-down model can best be built if in every layer of living stones there is a balance. This balance comes when we do not think of ourselves more highly than we ought, but think of ourselves with sober judgment in accordance with the measure of faith God has given us (see Romans 12:3-16). Further, in addition to the balance where the different members and gifts are balanced and each given the right place, the real strength and unity comes through relationship birthed and tied together with the bond of unconditional love which is the cement holding us together.

Unconditional love is important, because in this upside-down Kingdom, the least becomes the most important as the disciples had to learn: Luke 9:46-50: *"An argument started among the disciples as to which of them would be the greatest. Jesus, knowing their thoughts, took a little child and had him stand beside him. Then he said to them, 'Whoever welcomes this little child in my name welcomes me; and whoever welcomes me welcomes the one who sent me. For he who is least among you all – he is the greatest.' 'Master,' said John, 'we saw a man driving out demons in your name and we tried to stop him, because he is not one of us.' 'Do not stop him' Jesus said, 'for whoever is not against you is for you.'"*

The disciples had a hard time getting the concept, for Jesus had to deal with this many times and even on the night before the crucifixion as John recorded in John 13:1-17 when Jesus took the towel and the basin and washed their feet. Let us look closely at His teaching at the end of this passage: John 13:12-1: *"When he had finished washing their feet, he put on his clothes and returned* *to his place. 'Do you understand what I have done for you?' he asked them. 'You call me 'Teacher' and 'Lord,' and rightly so, for that is what I am. Now that I, your Lord and Teacher, have washed your feet, you also should wash one another's feet. <u>I have set you an example that you should do as I have done for you. I tell you the truth, no servant is greater than his master, nor is a messenger greater than the one who sent him. Now that you know these things, you will be blessed if you do them.</u>"*

Note the final verses. Jesus our apostle set the example for true apostolic leadership. This is what apostolic leadership is all about, for the word apostle in Greek means a sent one. We as apostolic (sent) people are not greater than the One who sent us, our apostle, Jesus. He ended this illustration of apostolic leadership with a promise: "<u>Now that you know these things, you will be blessed if you do them!</u>"

So, how did those who know these words follow through? To that we need to turn next.

CHURCH LEADERSHIP THROUGH THE CENTURIES

Introduction:

We do not have the time to trace this in any detail, but a brief summary tells the story. The early church followed the model of Jesus and we see that all over the pages of the New Testament, e.g. Paul who wrote to the Corinthians in 2 Corinthians 11:7-9:

> *"Was it a sin for me to lower myself in order to elevate you by preaching the gospel of God to you free of charge? I robbed other churches by receiving support from them so as to serve you. And when I was with you and needed something, I was not a burden to anyone, for the brothers who came from*

Macedonia supplied what I needed. I have kept myself from being a burden to you in any way, and will continue to do so."

As we read the New Testament and listen to the leaders, we sense a spirit of brokenness and humility as they served. This continued and the church grew amidst opposition and persecution. However, with the conversion of the Emperor Constantine in the 4th century, a major change took place. As we saw earlier in this booklet, the leadership structure changed and they imposed the worldly system of the Roman Empire onto the church with a hierarchy of clergy. In a word: Like Israel they rejected the Kingship of God and restored the human kingdom ideal. In no time palaces (called churches) with rulers wearing clerical robes and "crowns", with servants to serve them, took the stage and the blessing of Jesus no longer touched His body. In time repression and abuse became rampant and not even those who truly tried to serve God could stop the tide. Eventually the dark ages set in and the light of the world was scarcely visible. As knowledge of the Scriptures was lost due to illiteracy and the use of Latin, which few understood, people were kept in darkness. Leaders exercised control over the people through ignorance and fear. Clergy were able to keep the people in bondage and muzzle any opposition for centuries. The earthly kingship model often leads to control and abuse.

The key that broke this was the translation of Scripture. The control exercised by the leadership by keeping the people in ignorance is very pointedly illustrated by the quote from a letter from the Archbishop in England to the Pope in 1411 regarding John Wycliffe's translation of the Bible in the local English, which opened the door to ordinary people to recover the truth that would set them free:

> *"This Master John Wyclif translated from Latin into English – the Gospel that Christ gave to the clergy and doctors of the Church ..... so that by his means it has become vulgar and more open to laymen and women who can read than it usually is to quite learned clergy of good intelligence. And so the pearl of the Gospel is scattered abroad and trodden underfoot of swine"*
>
> *(The Cambridge History of the Bible, Volume 2, p.388.)*

The reformation tore this old wineskin of Roman Catholicism and it led to the formation of a number of new denominational structures. However, despite the fact that the reformers rediscovered the priesthood of the believer in the pages of scripture, the new structures that were set up simply partly democratized the earthly kingship model. Instead of a ruling king there was now a ruling king supported by a ruling body (appointed or elected) and even though it was an improvement in many ways, it fell far short of the model of Jesus.

Following the outpouring of the Spirit in Azusa Street in the early 1900's there was the birthing of the Pentecostal movement. Interestingly enough, in a very strange way many of the new charismatic churches not only set up structures similar to the ones from the Reformation, but more than most Protestant churches elevated the position of "pastor" to become yet again a priest placed on a pedestal. In fact, most charismatic churches apply the worldly kingship model in terms of leadership and the more independent charismatic churches treat this model as **the only model in Scripture!** E.g. the Pastor (Leadership) is seen as "the anointed" that may not be touched (criticized) and to whom all must submit. Those that follow the rules are then "covered" by the leadership and protected. There is also a very real lack of accountability in most cases – strangely covered up by the idea that as long as you belong to a wider group (mostly administrative) to whom you can point as "your covering" it is fine. Submission is enforced in subtle ways (often disguised spiritual abuse) or even in not so subtle ways with the preferred way of silencing a critic being to label him or her as "a Jezebel".

Submission to authority is the sacred cow in which we find the spirit of control that has destroyed many a fertile field. This sacred cow is supported by two golden calves and to those we need to turn next.

TOUCH NOT THE LORD'S ANOINTED

Introduction:

*A*s we noted above as we looked at the kingship model in the Old Testament, David had a number of opportunities to kill his rival and persecutor, Saul. In the cave at En Gedi David cut off a corner of Saul's robe, but then got conscience stricken and confessed that he had acted wrongly by lifting his hand against the Lord's anointed (1 Samuel 24:6). Two chapters later we read about another opportunity where David stopped his friend Abishai from killing a sleeping Saul, for he said it was not right to touch the Lord's anointed.

This concept is very much part and parcel of the independent charismatic churches where leadership and the pastor have been portrayed as "the anointed" and where criticism in any form against leadership decisions and styles are severely discouraged, as it would bring God's displeasure. It is used for most part to control the members of the church or fellowship and to keep them "in submission". (We find similar processes within the other denominations and as we continue, we will point these out). <u>The key problem is that this concept has its roots in the kingship model, which began as the rejection of God in favor of an earthly king like the other nations!</u>

David's dilemma:

David faced a real dilemma. God had rejected Saul and David was anointed to become king in his place. Within the pyramid of the kingship model there is only room for one at the top, so it was either he or Saul. Saul knew this and sought to kill him and as we have seen, David got some golden opportunities to kill his rival. However, if he did, he would set an example that could come back to haunt him or his successors. So, he chose to wait and not take the throne by force and it paid off as years later he did indeed become king. The problem was that others did not follow his example. His son, Absalom, did not hesitate to try and overthrow him and down in history the process was repeated many times.

The problem the king faced was that of keeping control over the people and to keep them in submission. Let us illustrate this with another example from Israel's history, recorded in 1 Kings 12. Solomon had died and after a rule with much repression (they paid the price that Samuel had warned them about in 1 Samuel 8!) the people met with his son Rehoboam who was to succeed him. They had a simple request: Lighten the burden and we will serve you. (By the way – note the fact that in the worldly kingdom the people serve the leader! This was what Jesus said should be turned upside down!) Having consulted with the wise elders and with his young friends, he chose to reject the request of the people and the advice of the elders. Instead of that he chose to threaten the people into submission. This led to a schism and the northern part of the kingdom broke away to form the Kingdom of Israel and it led to bloodshed and war. <u>Control often leads to pain and division.</u>

The newly formed Kingdom of Israel chose Jeroboam, a critic of Solomon's reign, to be their king. However, he faced the same problem of control. He needed to keep Israel from returning to Rehoboam and in this he faced a major obstacle. Under David Jerusalem had become the political and religious center. This was strengthened when Solomon built the temple. The dilemma Jeroboam faced and his response are described in 1 Kings 12:26-33. He had to provide an alternative to the power and attraction of Jerusalem and the temple. So, he set up golden calves – one in the south at Bethel and the other in the north at Dan. There he created sanctuaries of worship to keep the people from traveling to Jerusalem and from re-establishing the roots to David's throne. These golden calves were erected to support the sacred cow of regal authority.

How this functioned is very pointedly illustrated in the subsequent history of the northern Kingdom of Israel when Jeroboam II was king. God sent Amos as prophet to announce judgment over Israel. Amos traveled from the southern Kingdom of Judah to Bethel and prophesied at the sanctuary. Let us pick up the story in Amos 7:10-16:

> *"Then Amaziah the priest of Bethel sent a message to Jeroboam king of Israel: 'Amos is raising a conspiracy against you in the very heart of Israel. The land cannot bear his words. For this is what Amos is saying: 'Jeroboam will die by the sword and Israel will surely go into exile, away from their land.'*
>
> *Then Amaziah said to Amos: 'Get out, you seer. Go back to the land of Judah. Earn your bread there and do your prophesying there. Don't prophesy anymore at Bethel, because this is the king's sanctuary and the temple of the kingdom.'*
>
> *Amos answered Amaziah, 'I was neither a prophet nor a prophet's son, but I was a shepherd, and I also took care of sycamore-fig trees. But the Lord took me from tending the flock and said to me, 'Go, prophesy to my people Israel.' Now then, hear the word of the Lord: 'You say, 'Do not prophesy against Israel and stop preaching against the house of Isaac.' Therefore, this is what the Lord says, 'Your wife will become a prostitute in the city and your sons and daughters will fall by the sword. Your land will be measured and divided up and you your self will die in a pagan country. And Israel will certainly go into exile, away from their native land.'"*

The erection of the sanctuaries at Dan and Bethel with the idols served to support the spirit of control that was hidden behind the sacred cow of submission to the authority of the anointed king and his appointed priests. In a very similar way, the spirit of control has hidden behind the sacred cow of submission to the authority of church leadership through much of history. This sacred cow has depended on two golden calves to keep control. In the Roman Catholic system, the calves are tradition – particularly the tradition on the papal authority – and the sacraments. The latter are the tools handled exclusively by the clergy to maintain control. In the traditional protestant churches the calves are the doctrines and polities of the church and also the handling of the Word and sacraments by clergy. In the Pentecostal and independent charismatic churches, the sacred cow of submission to authority is upheld by the golden calves of the teachings about "touch not the Lord's anointed" and "covering".

Let us return to the story of Amos and apply it to our situation. Just imagine a modern-day Amos, e.g. a simple farmer from a small-town community who happens to be a Baptist entering a major Pentecostal church and walking up to the microphone during a service to deliver a message of correction to the church and leaders. Can you see the ushers removing him from the church and the pastor saying things like: "This word cannot be received? This man is totally out of order. Any directive word should be presented to the leadership first for review. Further, this man has no credentials. He is a no-name self-appointed prophet. He has not gone to any accredited school and worse still, he has no covering. He has brought judgment upon himself by speaking against the pastor and leadership for he has touched the Lord's anointed. He is no prophet at all!"

Let us push the envelope a little more! If Amos were to show up at your local church with the word of the Lord – would he have been given the opportunity to speak as he did or not? If he did get past the controls regarding prophetic words in the assembly, would his words have been received? **Let him who has an ear listen to what the Spirit is saying!**

Fear is a powerful mechanism to keep criticism from surfacing. Many submit because of fear and would not question the decisions of leaders, even things they know to be wrong. Many a move of God was derailed, because of fear of man.

The whole system of control is further maintained through the training at "approved academic schools" and by the bodies controlling credentials – in most denominational structures (including those who do not consider themselves denominational). Without the approved training and screening no one can step into the approved leadership roles and structures. This is a far cry from the simple on the job training model in the New Testament and it is no wonder we have powerless leaders ruling like mini popes and the sheep wandering around with no shepherd. The title "Pastor" with or without credentials does not make one a leader or a shepherd.

Even though in the general understanding of the Scriptures no charismatic believer or leader will outright deny that any spirit filled believer is anointed, there is a very strong belief that the pastor (or apostle or prophet) is "the anointed man of God."

This belief is upheld by teaching and many are literally scared to voice anything that could even remotely sound like criticism of leadership. It is very true that the Bible teaches the concept of submission to authority including the authority of leadership in the church, e.g. Hebrews 13:7: *"Remember your leaders, who spoke the word of God to you. Consider the outcome of their way of life and imitate their faith."*

However, it is not a one-way street! Submission is a general way of life for all believers and Paul wrote to the Ephesians that we should *"submit to one another out of reverence for Christ"* (Ephesians 5:21). We will come back to this again, but let us get to the heart of the issue.

The concept of the "Pastor" (Leader) as the anointed of God is rooted in the Old Testament kingship model. In the Old Testament only selected individuals were anointed, mostly priests (Leviticus 8), prophets and kings (e.g. 1 Kings 19:15-16). In the New Testament on the day of Pentecost the Holy Spirit was poured out on all in the upper room (Acts 2) and Peter explained this to the curious crowd that gathered outside in the words of the prophesy of Joel 2:28-29: *"And afterward, <u>I will pour out my Spirit on all people</u>. Your sons and daughters will prophesy, your old men will dream dreams, your young men will see visions.*

Even on my servants, both men and women, I will pour out my Spirit in those days."

It is for this reason that John wrote the following in 1 John 2:20 – 27: *"<u>But you have an anointing from the Holy One, and all of you know the truth</u>. I do not write to you because you do not know the truth, but because you do know it and because no lie comes from the truth. Who is the liar? It is the man who denies that Jesus is the Christ. Such a man is the antichrist – he denies the Father and the Son. No one who denies the Son has the Father; whoever acknowledges the Son has the Father also. See that what you have heard from the beginning remains in you. If it does, you also will remain in the Son and in the Father. And this is what he promised us – even eternal life. I am writing these things to you about those who are trying to lead you astray. <u>As for you, the anointing you received from him remains in you</u>, and you do not need anyone to teach you. <u>But as his anointing teaches you about all things and as that anointing is real, not counterfeit – just as it has taught you, remain in him</u>."*

Note that John literally says that the believers have the anointing and thus walk in the revealed truth. In the Kingdom of God those who are spirit filled have the anointing! **Each of us is God's anointed!** This is why we are to submit to one another. If we are not to touch the Lord's anointed <u>it means we are to be careful how we treat every other believer. It is not for leadership alone!</u>

Let us take it one step further: The concept of not touching the Lord's anointed originate in the Old Testament model of the kingship that started in rebellion against God's rule. Then Jesus turned this whole thing upside down as we have seen (e.g. Matthew 20:25-28). The leaders in this divine Kingdom model are not those who are more anointed and stand at the top lording it over the others, but are those who are willing to serve. In the kingdom of God, the first shall be last and the last first. The greatest is the least.

Listen to the words of Jesus recorded in Matthew 18:1-6:

> *"At that time the disciples came to Jesus and asked, 'Who is the greatest in the kingdom of heaven?' He called a little child and had him stand among them. And he said: 'I tell you the truth, unless you change and become like little children, you will never enter the kingdom of heaven. Therefore, whoever humbles himself like this child is the greatest in the kingdom of heaven.' And whoever welcomes a little child like this in my name welcomes me. But if anyone causes one of these little ones who believe in me to sin, it would be better for him to have a large millstone hung around his neck and to be drowned in the depths of the sea.'"*

The principle is this: If we cause any of the least (children in the natural or in the faith) to stumble, we have touched the Lord's anointed.

In this there is a major lesson and a warning to those in leadership in the church. It is best expressed in the words of Peter in 1 Peter 5:1-4: *"To the elders among you, I appeal as a fellow elder, a witness of Christ's sufferings and one who also will share in the glory to be revealed: Be shepherds of God's flock that is under your care, serving as overseers - not because you must, but because you are willing, as God wants you to be; not greedy for money, but eager to serve; not lording it over those entrusted to you, but being examples to the flock and when the Chief Shepherd appears, you will receive the crown of glory that will never fade away."*

Jesus also prayed a remarkable prayer recorded in Matthew 11:25 – 26 and then spoke words to put this prayer in context:

> Matthew 11:25-30: *"At that time Jesus said, <u>'I praise you Father, Lord of heaven and earth, because you have hidden these things from the wise and learned, and revealed them to little children</u>. Yes, Father, for this was your good pleasure. All things have been committed to me by my Father. No one knows the Son except the Father, and no one knows the Father except the Son and those to whom the Son chooses to reveal him. Come to me, all you who are weary and burdened, and I will give you rest. Take my yoke upon you and learn from me, for I am gentle and humble in heart and you will find rest for your souls for my yoke is easy and my burden is light."*

In many of our churches where there is openness for the move of the Spirit, we miss that the revelation and word of God can come and often does come through the most unlikely vessels. The sad part is that leaders more often than not never release the revelation because of the control, especially if there is any correction in the word. The control of the prophetic word by leaders "who judge the word from their position of special anointing" is little else but spiritual pride and arrogance. <u>It is no different than the quote regarding Wycliffe's translation of the Scriptures by the archbishop in 1411 – except that</u>

<u>in this case it is the Rhema word being controlled by the modern-day priests, called "pastors"!</u>

One of the greatest tragedies in the church is the way that many prophetic people who are called "intercessors" have been persecuted by leaders because they shared what God had revealed to them. We have personally had the privilege to minister to many who have been abused and burdened in this way. Often they had been labeled "Jezebels" as the word of God was shared with leadership that did not like the word, just like Amaziah did with the words Amos spoke forth at Bethel. Interestingly enough, few ever acknowledge that the Jezebel spirit is a ruling spirit operating most prominently through those in leadership just like the woman who personified the spirit, queen Jezebel. Also, this spirit predominantly attacks the prophets of God as Jezebel did with Elijah and the prophets in those days. **Therefore, the first place to seek and find the Jezebel spirit is in the key leadership in a church and it is revealed most often in the way the prophetic words are being handled!**

It is time that the golden calf called "touch not the Lord's anointed leader" is destroyed so that the Kingdom of God can come in many a church. This calf has done nothing but support the sacred cow of submission to the worldly model of kingdom authority in which the Jezebel spirit of control is hiding. With that we need to move on to the other golden calf called "Covering".

COVERING

The concept of covering is mostly used in independent charismatic circles and implies a spiritual protection by submission to leadership. From a positive point of view, it is an attempt to have accountability in ministry. Within this there is a recognition that it is not good to be a lone ranger and we need to be accountable. In the traditional denominations the denominational leadership structures and church polities are to serve the same purpose. Submission to authority in this way provides a protective cover and support to us.

Tied into this package is the recognition that authority comes when we walk under authority as illustrated in the story of the Roman Centurion in Luke 7:1-10:

> *When Jesus had finished saying all this in the hearing of the people, he entered Capernaum. There a centurion's servant, whom his master valued highly, was sick and about to die. The centurion heard of Jesus and sent some elders of the Jews to him, asking him to come and heal his servant. When they*

came to Jesus, they pleaded earnestly with him, "This man deserves to have you do this, because he loves our nation and has built our synagogue." So Jesus went with them.

He was not far from the house when the centurion sent friends to say to him: "Lord, don't trouble yourself, for I do not deserve to have you come under my roof. That is why I did not even consider myself worthy to come to you. But say the word, and my servant will be healed. For I myself am a man under authority, with soldiers under me. I tell this one, `Go,' and he goes; and that one, `Come,' and he comes. I say to my servant, `Do this,' and he does it."

When Jesus heard this, he was amazed at him, and turning to the crowd following him, he said, "I tell you, I have not found such great faith even in Israel." Then the men who had been sent returned to the house and found the servant well.

Using this story as example many have been taught that as they submit to the authority of the leadership or pastor, they will walk in authority and under a spiritual protection called "covering". Thus, release into ministry and authority to minister depend upon one's submission to the anointed authority of the pastor and leaders. In this a high priority is placed upon submission and the anointing is said to flow down from the anointed leadership onto those who walk in submission and are in unity as described in Psalm 133:

"How good and pleasant it is when brothers live together in unity! It is like precious oil poured on the head, running down on the beard, running down on Aaron's beard, down upon the collar of his robes. It is as if the dew of Hermon were falling

on Mount Zion. For there the Lord bestows his blessing, even life forevermore."

Therefore, walking under the authority of anointed leadership in unity with one another brings a blessing as the anointing flows down from the top. The opposite is also taught: If one does not submit to the anointed authority (our other golden calf), one brings a curse upon oneself and the door to ministry is closed. After all, without submission one cannot have authority and the anointing to minister.

Before we look at the real truths buried in the mix and how they should be applied, we need to consider an important issue. The Roman Centurion understood authority. He walked under the authority of the Emperor and as someone under authority he understood that his authority came from the authority vested in him by his submission to the Emperor. Note that this understanding came from the kingship model and it is correct. However, he also recognized in Jesus an authority that the worldly model did not have. He saw in Jesus a spiritual authority and knew that Jesus walked under the authority of God. This was an authority that no man could give anyone! Jesus' authority is the authority that came from his submission to God the Father and this kind of authority is released only as one walks in submission to God. As Son of God, Jesus chose to obey the Father and come to this earth and as Son of man He walked in obedience all the way to death on the cross (Philippians 2:6-11). In His own words: John

6:38: *"For I have come down from heaven not to do my will but to do the will of him who sent me."*

The real issue is not just one of authority, but rather than that, it is the source of one's authority. This was the issue that brought Jesus in conflict with the religious leaders of His day e.g. John 2:18 and Matthew 21:23-27. The same issue came up again when the apostles were persecuted e.g. *Acts 4:7: "They had Peter and John brought before them and began to question them: 'By what power (authority) or what name did you do this?'"*

Let us cut to the heart of the matter. The real issue is one of control disguised as submission to human authority in the form of the worldly kingship model. The sacred cow of submission to authority, hiding the spirit of control. has effectively used this golden calf to keep many in submission and bondage. To understand this, we need to go to an old story recorded in Exodus 32. While Moses was on the mountain receiving the word of God, the Israelites asked Aaron to make a golden calf to represent God for them to worship. They paid a heavy price, for the resources they got as they left the slavery in Egypt were surrendered to create this idol. In the end they lost it all as Moses destroyed the idol and returned to Mount Sinai to again receive copies of the Ten Commandments. When he returned his face was radiant and because they could not look at him because of the radiance, he covered his face with a veil. In time though the radiance faded, but Moses kept his face covered so that they would not see that the radiance was gone.

In a similar way, many in the church have paid a very high price as they sought a human to provide a spiritual covering. Many times we are no different than the Israelites who wanted someone else to represent them before God and God before them. However, this is not necessary, because every one of us has the privilege to enter into the presence of God and to have an intimate relationship with him. Jesus is our example. He walked in submission to God and intimacy with God and thus in divine authority. More than that: He opened the door for us to have the same intimacy and authority as He had when we submit to God. The veil was torn to allow us to enter into the presence of God with boldness. Listen to this: Hebrews 10:19-22: *"Therefore, brothers, since we have confidence to enter the Most Holy Place by the blood of Jesus, by a new and living way opened for us through the curtain, that is, his body and since we have a great priest over the house of God, let us draw near to God, with a sincere heart in full assurance of faith, having our hearts sprinkled to cleanse us from a guilty conscience and having our bodies washed with pure water."*

However, we often prefer to have some other person pay the price and would willingly submit to them as they promise to represent us. Without thinking many have exchanged the spiritual protection that only God can give for a human protection and submitted to a human covering. We quickly bow to a godly leader like Moses and seek the comfort of being close to such a man or woman. To many the issue of covering has become their security blanket and they have a hard time seeing through the veil. To really grasp this let us read how Paul described the contrast between the old model of leadership and the freedom in the Kingdom of God when we simply enter into the intimate relationship with Jesus and walk in faith under his divine covering and in fellowship with one another.

<u>2 Corinthians 3:7-18:</u> *"Now if the ministry that brought death, which was engraved in letters on stone, came with glory, so that the Israelites could not look steadily at the face of Moses because of its glory, fading though it was, will not the ministry of the Spirit be even more glorious? If the ministry that condemns men is glorious, how much more glorious is the ministry that brings righteousness! For what was glorious has no glory now in comparison with the surpassing glory. And if what was fading away came with glory, how much greater is the glory of that which lasts! Therefore, since we have such a hope, we are very bold. We are not like Moses, who would put a veil over his face to keep the Israelites from gazing at it while the radiance was fading away. But their minds were made dull, for to this day the same veil remains when the old covenant is read. It has not been removed, because only in Christ is it taken away. Even to this day when Moses is read, a veil covers their hearts. But whenever anyone turns to the Lord, the veil is taken away. Now the Lord is the Spirit, and where the Spirit of the Lord is, there is freedom. And we, who with unveiled faces all reflect the Lord's glory, are being transformed into his likeness with ever-increasing glory, which comes from the Lord, who is the Spirit."*

Let us look at this in the light of the two leadership models. The worldly kingship model opens the door for a human covering. It calls for a hierarchic pyramid structure. I can only cover someone if I am over them and standing on a higher level. Only by being at the top of the pyramid can anyone cover the others. This is why this issue is taught mostly in circles where this Old Testament kingship model is seen as the ideal Biblical model for the church's leadership. Jesus' model of the leader as servant will never lead to the leader becoming a covering for someone. You do not cover people if you are serving them and lifting them up.

Further, if I do cover anyone that very cover will be a barrier between the person and God. By asking any person, however anointed, to be my covering, I have chosen to have someone between God and me. In the light of that let us read Psalm 91:1-13:

> *"He who dwells in the shelter of the Most High will rest in the shadow of the Almighty.*
>
> *I will say of the Lord, 'He is my refuge and my fortress, my God, in whom I trust,'*
>
> *surely he will save you from the fowler's snare and from the deadly pestilence.*
>
> *He will cover you with his feathers, and under his wings you will find refuge;*
>
> *his faithfulness will be your shield and rampart.*
>
> *You will not fear the terror of night, nor the arrow that flies by day, nor the pestilence that stalks in the darkness, nor the plague that destroys at midday.*

> *A thousand may fall at your side, ten thousand at your right hand, but it will not come near you. You will only observe with your eyes and see the punishment of the wicked.*
>
> *If you make the Most High your dwelling – even the Lord, who is my refuge – then no harm will befall you, no disaster will come near your tent. For he will command his angels concerning you to guard you in all your ways; they will lift you up in their hands, so that you will not strike your foot against a stone. You will tread upon the lion and the cobra; you will trample the great lion and the serpent."*

Having read that, could I ask you as reader a simple question? If you have the choice (and you do) to have me or any other person be your spiritual covering or have God himself be that, why in the world would you not choose God? The security blanket called covering is nothing else than a veil keeping us from seeing God. It is no different than the traditions of Israel or the traditions and polities of the traditional churches that likewise keep people from entering into God's presence.

Let us consider Paul's words in the end of 2 Corinthians 3. When we turn to the Lord, we do not want coverings over us. We want every veil removed. <u>The real task of leadership is not to cover people, but to help them to break through every veil and enter into the presence of our Lord with unveiled faces!</u> We do not need any human shadows to cloud our vision. It is in the presence of God that we are set free! True freedom is to get rid of all the human trappings of power and move under the protection of God. <u>There is no greater freedom than to be covered by the Spirit of the living God and to walk</u>

under that anointing. It is in that place where we begin to reflect the glory of God and our faces begin to be transformed from glory to glory. As leaders we ought to seek to break every covering off so that every person can reflect the glory radiating from the divine glory covering us. We need to get out of the way between God and those entrusted to our care and lift them higher into the presence of God.

When we really read the Word, we will find that within the Bible the term "covering" is not used in the sense described above. It is used as physical clothing or a shelter. In the New Testament this term refers mostly to the issue of a woman's head cover and we do not wish to enter into that debate here! There is no place in the New Testament where this term is ever used to describe a spiritual protection offered to any person submitting to a human spiritual leader! Our authority and our protection are from God alone. This is what we need to teach and allow the freedom of the Spirit to be released in the church. **The very concept of covering as it is applied in many churches is nothing more than an idol that provides a cover to insecure leadership to hide the spirit of control.**

The story about the centurion needs to be seen for what it is. The centurion walked under the authority of the greatest human power of his day, the Roman Emperor. His submission to Caesar did not give him the anointing needed to help his servant! He came to Jesus, who was a no name in the worldly power circles, but he recognized that Jesus walked under the authority of God and had the anointing he did not have. Jesus had the power to heal his servant with one word! Your anointing will be according to the authority under whom you submit and you can choose to walk under divine authority anointed by the Spirit or in the power of the flesh by bowing to human leadership.

The kingship model has had a devastating effect upon the members of the church and it continues to this day. However, it has also taken a heavy toll on the leadership. To this we need to turn next.

CRITICISM AND REBELLION

The North American Church and many churches in other parts of the world have accepted the worldly kingship model in one form or another as the Biblical model for church leadership. We have seen how this model has caused major hurt and pain to many in the pews. However, most in church leadership positions are wonderful people who are committed and caring. The roots of the problem are not the current leaders even though there are exceptions. The roots are in the model itself, because it began in rebellion against God. Having been birthed in rebellion, this model is an open door for the spirit of rebellion and its brother, the spirit of criticism.

It began the moment the first king of Israel was anointed. Directly following the anointing of Saul, we read: 1 Samuel 10:27: *"But some troublemakers said, 'How can this fellow save us?' They despised him and brought him no gifts."*

As the kingship story continued, this happened again and again. As Saul persecuted David we read an interesting note: 1 Samuel 22:2: *"All those who were in distress or in debt <u>or discontented</u> gathered around David and he became their leader."*

Among those who supported David was Joab. He became the commander of David's forces, but had a rebellious and violent spirit that caused David major problems, e.g. when he and his brother murdered Abner (See 2 Samuel 3:22-39). In time David's own son Absalom rebelled and tried to overthrow him and with him were many in Israel. We have also seen that following Solomon's death, the northern part of the Kingdom broke away and the leader was Jeroboam who was a critic of Solomon.

The very history of the church is likewise a story of the criticism and rebellion resulting in division. It started when the Roman Empire's model of leadership was imposed upon the church under Constantine and has continued to this day. Incidentally, this is the model that the Roman Centurion found wanting when he came to Jesus! Most of these roots are inherent in the structure of the church's leadership as the worldly kingship model is applied to the leadership. This structure is an open door for insecure leaders to allow the spirits of control and fear of failure to take over leading to abuse. On the other hand, as it was birthed in the rejection of God's rule, it is also an open door to spirits of criticism, rebellion and rejection of leaders to enter into the church.

This is why the North American Church is in such turmoil and decline. Many pastors who are good men and women burn out and leave the pastorate. The average length of a pastorate is between 2-4 years and if the pastor survives the turbulence beyond 4 years it is often only because the main critics leave. Church splits are a way of life in our society because there is a rebellious spirit in the North American Church. Many a pastor and many pastoral families have been devastated by the rebellious attitudes of members – just as controlling pastors have hurt many members. The spirits of control and rebellion work together in order to destroy the work of the Kingdom. Another major problem is the fact that the accepted model sees the office as pastor as a resident leader in the church. The only place in the New Testament where the term 'pastor' is used referring to an office is in Ephesians 4:12 and here it is one of the 5 offices. The task of the pastor is not to pastor a local church, but to be part of itinerant teams to equip the members of the local churches for their ministry of pastoring! The oversight and pastoring in the local church is the task of the mature leaders recognized in their gifts and appointed as elders and this leadership is always entrusted to a plurality of elders. The current accepted church leadership model flows from the unbiblical division of the body into clergy and laity and leads to the usurping of the leadership of the local mature leaders by the appointed professional and is birthed in division! Small wonder there is such a leadership crisis in the church! It does not matter what title is used – pastor, minister, priest, bishop or apostle

– resident clergy is not Scriptural and will continue to lead to problems!

In this there is a warning to those who move into the renewal and seeking to restore the apostolic church. Most of the leading apostolic leaders and churches have not addressed this issue. It is particularly important, as there has been a key connection between the church growth movement and the new apostolic churches in North America. Most of the new apostolic churches are steeped in a theology that accepts the kingship model as the Biblical model for church leadership. The bigger the church the more likely the leader is to be accepted as an apostle. No doubt many are, but the North American model of church growth only needs a good administrator with management skills who knows how to cater to a consumer society to build a mega church. **If those who are on the leading edge of renewal do not address this issue, the building will not stand the test of time. Servant leadership cannot be applied from the top. The pope is called "the servant of servants" – but the reality is that he is on the top of the pyramid and this is diametrically opposite of Jesus' leadership. In the same way can no apostle rule from the top.**

This is why Jesus said that the old wineskin would not hold the new wine. The structure has to be radically changed. Much of the current renewal has not touched the structure of the church in a radical way. We have tried to repair the cracks in the wall and even to patch a leaky foundation. We keep cutting the new garment to patch the old and it may be very colorful, but we need to discard the old and put on the new garment. If we just build new mega churches and have a great time of worship and run the programs, we have not changed anything! Covering up the cracks is not the answer. We need a radical shift in leadership models and accepting the fivefold offices is not the answer, especially if they are applied to the wrong model of leadership. True servant leadership is absolutely essential to equip and release the members into their ministry. It is from below and will lift the members up and encourage and release them. It will lead to true relationship, which is the soil in which accountability and oversight thrive.

Accountability and oversight are very important, but again the Biblical model will show that these issues were not handled through the concept of submission to a covering (or to ecclesiastical structures) as we have today. The way these were handled came out of personal relationships that led to a network of churches where those who were called to leadership led through example and earned the right to speak into the lives of the individuals and churches. To this we need to turn next.

FOUNDATIONS OF COVENANT RELATIONSHIPS

Introduction:

*G*od is in the process of restoring the church to its foundations – or in the picture of Luke 5:37-38, He is pouring out the new wine and the old wineskins will not work. What we can see develop are networks of interdependent churches, many home-based, tied together through **covenant relationship** based on a shared vision.

As the vision is unfolding, we will find more and more who come to be part of the vision. It is foundational that we clarify the principles of the relationships needed and the steps leading to covenant relationships. This applies not just to the relationships between the churches and leaders and between the network and overseers, but also to the relationship between those attending the house churches and the local leadership.

Let us look at the process to develop these covenant relationships in terms of two pictures that may not seem to belong together, but work well to illustrate it: Playing baseball and getting married!

1. **Taking the first step:**

    As believers we are in the game of life – and we are on the winning team! There are many teams in the league. Joining an apostolic network is like choosing to play on a certain team under certain coaches. The first step in the process is a decision to begin to walk in this relationship and if followed through it will get us to first base. It is the same as asking someone on a date with the intention of more dates to follow – and expecting that this might be the one that you will marry.

    Proverbs 18:24: *"A man of many companions may come to ruin, but there is a friend who sticks closer than a brother."*

    Amos 3:3: *"Do two walk together unless they have agreed to do so?"*

    Ecclesiastes 4:9-12: *"Two are better than one, because they have a good return for their work: If one falls down, his friend can help him up. But pity the man who falls and has no one to help him up! Also, if two lie down together, they will keep warm. But how can one keep warm alone? Though one may be overpowered, two can defend themselves. A cord of three strands is not quickly broken."*

The key is to seek agreement and it is also vital to know that God is in it!

e.g. Acts 16:6-10: *"Paul and his companions traveled throughout the region of Phrygia and Galatia, having been kept by the Holy Spirit from preaching the word in the province of Asia. When they came to the border of Mysia, they tried to enter Bithynia, but the Spirit of Jesus would not allow them to. So they passed by Mysia and went down to Troas. During the night Paul had a vision of a man of Macedonia standing and begging him, 'Come over to Macedonia and help us.' After Paul had seen the vision, we got ready at once to leave for Macedonia, concluding that God had called us to preach the gospel to them.*

Note that Paul and his companions sought to minister in certain areas and kept finding the doors closed. Through a divine revelation they recognized the open door into Europe and set out fully expecting that there will be divine connections. They were not disappointed as God set up the divine connection with Lydia and it led to a church being planted.

This is precisely the strategy Jesus had when he sent out the 12 and later the 72 as we read in Luke 9:1-6 and Luke 10:1-12:

> *When Jesus had called the Twelve together, he gave them power and authority to drive out all demons and to cure diseases, and he sent them out to preach the kingdom of*

God and to heal the sick. He told them: "Take nothing for the journey-no staff, no bag, no bread, no money, no extra tunic. <u>Whatever house you enter, stay there until you leave that town. If people do not welcome you, shake the dust off your feet when you leave their town, as a testimony against them." So they set out and went from village to village, preaching the gospel and healing people everywhere.</u>

After this the Lord appointed seventy-two others and sent them two by two ahead of him to every town and place where he was about to go. He told them, "The harvest is plentiful, but the workers are few. Ask the Lord of the harvest, therefore, to send out workers into his harvest field. Go! I am sending you out like lambs among wolves. Do not take a purse or bag or sandals; and do not greet anyone on the road.

<u>When you enter a house, first say, `Peace to this house.' If a man of peace is there, your peace will rest on him; if not, it will return to you. Stay in that house, eating and drinking whatever they give you, for the worker deserves his wages. Do not move around from house to house.</u>

When you enter a town and are welcomed, eat what is set before you. Heal the sick who are there and tell them, `The kingdom of God is near you.' But when you enter a town and are not welcomed, go into its streets and say, `Even the dust of your town that sticks to our feet we wipe off against you. Yet be sure of this: The kingdom of God is near.' I tell you, it will be more bearable on that day for Sodom than for that town."

Let us apply this for a moment. The first step to network is to move in response to the doors God open and to seek the divine appointments. These can be new converts or believers called to open their home or business. Apostolic teams then begin to work with these people and explore the vision God has given and encourage the formation of the church. Today in the west we often find that the church is already functioning and just needs to be encouraged and networked. Initially the relationship will be less intense as it needs time to develop. **This means we are about on first base – dating occasionally.**

If it stays here – we may enjoy it, but in baseball terms, you do not win by getting players on first base! If you only keep dating, you will never get married! It is like someone coming to a fellowship once or twice a month.

2. **Taking the next step:**

To move to second base a deeper commitment is necessary. It is like two people deciding to not just date, but go steady. You are not yet engaged, but now working towards that. It is purposely choosing to pursue a deeper relationship.

Let us talk about that in terms of the objective of the fivefold ministry: The apostles and others leaders are given to equip and release the members for their ministry (see Eph. 4:12). The first connection is usually with the leadership or potential leaders to support and strengthen them and to impart the apostolic anointing and stir up gifts. Within the bigger vision apostolic teams work to build a network of key leaders and churches that interconnect and support and help one another. Therefore, they visit regularly and in time send key leaders to visit the home churches and help them in the small setting. At the same time, the home churches step out and support the celebration services and leadership events led by apostolic teams where they join with others in a bigger setting. If the home church leaders do not see it as a priority to join with the other leaders at the leadership events, we will not move beyond first base. It is in these larger gatherings where there is a different atmosphere and anointing. Coming together in such gatherings the members are encouraged and receive impartation from the others and particularly from those flowing in the fivefold ministry gifts. There is a cross pollination as these churches gather together.

If a church and its leaders only focus on the local vision, the net will be weakened at that point and might break. We need to have the net strong to gather the harvest. The word 'equip' used in Ephesians 4:12 to describe the work of the fivefold ministries is the same Greek word used in the gospels to describe the mending of the nets by John and James (Mark 1:19) – and the object is to have a net that will hold the end-time catch! **The end time harvest will only come about through the no-names that have been equipped and**

released to reach their local communities interconnecting with others in the wider community.

Let us look at the story in Acts 16:13-15 to see how this worked.

> *"On the Sabbath, we went outside the city gate to the river, where we expected to find a place of prayer. We sat down and began to speak to the women who had gathered there. One of those listening was a woman named Lydia, a dealer in purple cloth from the city of Thyatira, who was a worshiper of God. The Lord opened her heart to respond to Paul's message. When she and the members of her household were baptized, she invited us to her home. 'If you consider me a believer in the Lord,' she said, 'come and stay at my house.' And she persuaded us."*

Once Lydia opened her heart, she was baptized and then she opened her home and her resources. That home became the base for the church in Philippi. She chose to develop a deeper relationship with the visiting apostolic team and began investing in them and in their vision.

It is vital that after the first step a decision is made to go to the next level and invest in the relationship – and make it a priority. This is not a one-way street. The house church invests in the support of the apostolic team, while the team invests in the equipping of the members for their work of ministry! But again – if that is where it stays, it is little different than stranding a runner at second base. It does not win the game!

3. **<u>Paying the price:</u>**

Once on second base, we need to move the runner to third base! Going steady does not get you married. You need to pay the price and get the ring! It calls for a new level of commitment. This next level is the place where you invest yourself and your resources. Let me give you an example from Paul's life found in his letter to Philemon. Philemon was a friend in Colosse and had a good relationship with Paul. The issue raised in this letter was a slave of Philemon by the name of Onesimus. He ran away from his master and God set up a divine appointment where this slave met Paul and became a believer and proved to be a great help to Paul. However, as a run-away slave he was illegally with Paul and so Paul wrote this letter and sent him back to his master with it. In the letter he asked Philemon to forgive Onesimus and allow him to return with his blessing to help Paul in ministry.

Let us look at the relationship and the tone of Paul's request: Paul did not take the relationship with Philemon for granted. He asked Philemon to do these things, even though as Apostle and friend, he could command! He had an open door at Philemon's house and hospitality was guaranteed there whenever he visited Colosse, but he respectfully asked the favor. He expected a yes! There is a courtesy and respect throughout Paul's letter and it reflects the relationship they had as brothers. We also see this in the fact that <u>they prayed for one another</u>:

> Philemon 4-6 and 22: *"I always thank my God as I remember you in <u>my prayers</u>, because I hear about your faith in the Lord Jesus and your love for all the saints. I pray that you may be active in sharing your faith, so that you will have a full understanding of every good thing we have in Christ."*

> v22: *"And one thing more: Prepare a guest room for me, because I hope to be restored to you in answer to <u>your prayers</u>."*

Philemon also networked – through Paul: Verses 23-24: *"Epaphras, my fellow prisoner in Christ Jesus, sends you greetings. And so do Mark, Aristarchus, Demas and Luke, my fellow workers."*

As we pursue the Biblical model for apostolic networks, we need to develop relationships where we make commitments regarding finances and resources. Remember Lydia: She opened her home and a church was planted. As Lydia opened her home and resources to Paul and his friends, it let to the next step and this church poured into Paul's ministry whenever they could. Philippians 4:10-19: *"I rejoice greatly in the Lord that at last you have renewed your concern for me. Indeed, you have been concerned, but you had no opportunity to show it. I am not saying this because I am in need, for I have learned to be content whatever the circumstances. I know what it is to be in need, and I know what it is to have plenty. I have learned the secret of being content in any and every situation, whether well fed or hungry, whether living in plenty or in want. I can do everything through him who gives me strength. Yet it was good of you to share in my troubles. Moreover, as you Philippians know, in the early days of your acquaintance with the gospel, when I set out from Macedonia, not one church shared with me in the matter of giving and receiving, except you only; for even when I was in Thessalonica, you sent me aid again and again when I was in need. Not that I am looking for a gift, but I am looking for what may be credited to your account. I have received full payment and even more: I am amply supplied, now that I have received from Epaphroditus the gifts you sent. They are a fragrant offering, and acceptable sacrifice, pleasing to God. And my God will meet all your needs according to his glorious riches in Christ Jesus."*

As relationships deepen, we reach a level where we commit to sacrifice for the broader Kingdom vision and put our money and resources where our mouths are. This is where not only the local church, but also the individual members begin to pay the price to personally invest. Let me give you an illustration – a painful one at that: Acts 16:1-5: *"He came to Derbe and then to Lystra, where a disciple named Timothy lived, whose mother was a Jewess and a believer, but whose father was a Greek. The brothers at Lystra and Iconium spoke well of him. Paul wanted to take him along on the journey, so he circumcised him because of the Jews who lived in that area, for they all knew that his father was a Greek. As they traveled from town to town, they delivered the decisions reached by the apostles and elders in Jerusalem for the people to obey. So the churches were strengthened in the faith and grew daily in numbers."*

Timothy agreed to circumcision for the gospel's sake! He did not have to do this and Paul did not normally expect that of anyone – but in this case it could eliminate some obstacles to reach the Jews and Timothy agreed for the sake of Paul's vision to reach the community! It went both ways: Paul personally invested in developing Timothy and raising him as a leader – and when equipped he released him in a major way, e.g.

1 Corinthians 4:17: *"For this reason I am sending to you Timothy, my son whom I love, who is faithful in the Lord. He will remind you of my way of life in Christ Jesus, which agrees with what I teach everywhere in every church."*

and 1 Timothy 1:3: *"As I urged you when I went into Macedonia, stay there in Ephesus so that you may command certain men not to teach false doctrines any longer ...."*

There is a point at which the church and the leadership need to choose to commit to invest on a regular basis in the bigger vision of the network. To build the Kingdom vision and the Network is more than simply fellowship – even if it is good fellowship. As they invest in the bigger picture, they can expect that the apostolic leaders and network partners will invest to a greater

degree in developing and equipping the leaders and members of the local church. Like Paul, true apostolic leaders, help to equip local leaders e.g. by taking them with the apostolic teams on missions and opening doors for them to minister with key people to receive impartation and training. It has to be a two-way street. But again, if we stop here, we strand the runner on third base and in baseball it makes no difference if we strand a runner on first or second or third base! You have to reach home plate to score. Likewise – you can wear the engagement ring for years, but what you really want is to add the marriage ring! The objective is to get to a point where we formalize the relationship and enter into a binding covenant relationship! **That is where the real net is interconnected and prepared to land the big catch!**

4. **Entering the covenant relationship:**

Now, do you know where we mostly find information about this in Scripture? It is in the personal notes from Paul and others in the letters! It is in the personal notes, for the whole foundation of an apostolic network is relational. Let me show you how Paul built the network that is the true model of the fivefold ministry!

Let us go again to the letter to the church in Philippi and read Philippians 1:1-8: *"Paul and Timothy, servants of Christ Jesus, to all the saints in Christ Jesus at Philippi, together with the overseers and deacons: Grace and peace to you from God our Father and the Lord Jesus Christ. I thank my God every time I remember you. In all my prayers for all of you, I always pray with joy because of your partnership in the gospel from the first day until now, being confident of this, that he who began a good work in you will carry it on to completion until the day of Christ Jesus. It is right for me to feel this way about all of you, since I have you in my heart; for whether I am in chains or defending and confirming the gospel, all of you share in God's grace with me. God can testify how I long for all of you with the affection of Christ Jesus."*

Note that the Philippians stuck with him through thick and thin. Like we say when we commit to marry someone: "For better or worse, richer or poorer, in sickness and in health, until death us do part!" Also note that there is an apostolic finishing anointing on this: *"He who began the good work in us will complete it!"* Further note that Paul first greeted the no-names and then the overseers and deacons and note the love and affection as he writes!

That kind of relationship also opens the door for the times when we face discipline and tough decisions. Paul was tough at times – but he earned the right to speak into the life of the churches through relationship, e.g. 2 Corinthians 13:1-6: *"This will be my third visit to you. 'Every matter must be established by the testimony of two or three witnesses.' I already gave you a warning when I was with you the second time. I now repeat it while absent: On my return I will not spare those who sinned earlier or any of the others, since you are demanding proof that Christ is speaking through me. He is not weak in dealing with you, but is powerful among you. For to be sure, he was crucified in weakness, yet he lives by God's power. Likewise, we are weak in him, yet by God's power we will live with him to serve you. Examine yourselves to see whether you are in the faith; test yourselves. Do you not realize that Christ Jesus is in you – unless, of course, you fail the test? And I trust that you will discover that we have not failed the test."*

And also 1 Corinthians 5:3: *"Even though I am not physically present, I am with you in spirit. And I have already passed judgment on the one who did this, just as if I were present."*

The apostolic leaders had no problem stepping in and appointing leaders and Paul not only did it (Acts 14:21-23), but he also instructed leaders to help others belonging to the network e.g. Titus 3:12-14: *"As soon as I send Artemas or Tychicus to you, do your best to come to me at Nicopolis, because I have decided to winter there. Do everything you can to help Zenas the lawyer and Apollos on their way and see that they have everything they need. Our people must learn to devote themselves to doing what is good, in order that they may provide for daily necessities and not live unproductive lives."*

Prayer adds strength to the relationships. Remember when Jesus turned the tables and He said that the church should be a house of prayer for all nations. When we read Paul's letters, we read this everywhere. He prayed for everyone and every church so did those with him too and he expected them to pray for him and the other churches e.g.

> Ephesians 6:18-20: *"And pray in the Spirit on all occasions with all kinds of prayers and requests. With this in mind, be alert and always keep on praying for all the saints. Pray also for me, that whenever I open my mouth, words may be given me so that I will fearlessly make known the mystery of the gospel, for which I am an ambassador in chains. Pray that I may declare it fearlessly, as I should."*

> Colossians 4:2-4: *"Devote yourselves to prayer, being watchful and thankful. And pray for us too, that God may open a door for our message, so that we may proclaim the mystery of Christ, for which I am in chains. Pray that I may proclaim it clearly, as I should."*

> And Colossians 4:12-13: *"Epaphras, who is one of you and a servant of Christ Jesus, sends greetings. He is always wrestling in prayer for you, that you may stand firm in all the will of God, mature and fully assured. I vouch for him that he is working hard for you and for those at Laodicea and Hierapolis."*

> 1 Thessalonians 5:25: *"Brothers, pray for us."*

> and 2 Thessalonians 3:1-2: *"Finally, brothers, pray for us that the message of the Lord may spread rapidly and be honored, just as it was with you. And pray that we may be delivered from wicked and evil men, for not everyone has faith."*

They shared the Network news regarding the Kingdom, progress and needs with the churches and leaders, e.g.:

> Colossians 4:7-9: *"Tychicus will tell you all the news about me. He is a dear brother, a faithful minister and fellow servant in the Lord. I am sending him to you for the express purpose that you may know about our circumstances and that he may encourage your hearts. He is coming with Onesimus, our faithful and dear brother, who is one of you. They will tell you everything that is happening here."*
>
> Ephesians 6:21: *"Tychicus, the dear brother and faithful servant in the Lord, will tell you everything, so that you also may know how I am and what I am doing."*

Likewise, Paul and Barnabus with Silas and Judas were sent to deliver the letter and explain the decision of the Apostolic Council to the churches (Acts 15:23-35). The authority of the Apostles and leaders was birthed in relationship and submission to such authority earned through servant leadership, is to be expected (as Timothy showed by submitting to circumcision – Ouch!)

In the same way the covenant relationships opened the door for the apostolic workers. The churches had no problems receiving traveling workers and offering them support and hospitality. It was a given in the church e.g.:

Acts 18:1-3: *"After this, Paul left Athens and went to Corinth. There he met a Jew named Aquila, a native of Pontus, who had recently come from Italy with his wife Priscilla, because Claudius had ordered all the Jews to leave Rome. Paul went to see them, and because he was a tentmaker as they were, he stayed and worked with them."*

Acts 21:3-4: *"After sighting Cyprus and passing to the south of it, we sailed on to Syria. We landed at Tyre, where our ship was to unload its cargo. Finding the disciples there, we stayed with them seven days. Through the Spirit they urged Paul not to go on to Jerusalem."*

Acts 28:13-15: *"From there we set sail and arrived at Rhegium. The next day the south wind came up, and on the following day we reached Puteoli. There we found some brothers who invited us to spend a week with them. And so we came to Rome. The brothers there had heard that we were coming, and they traveled as far as the Forum of Appius and the Three Taverns to meet us. At the sight of these men Paul thanked God and was encouraged."*

Paul did not only receive hospitality and support as apostle, but he expected the church to receive and welcome those sent by him, e.g.:

1 Corinthians 16:10-11: *"If Timothy comes, see to it that he has nothing to fear while he is with you, for he is carrying on the work of the Lord, just as I am. No one, then, should refuse to accept him. Send him on his way in peace so that he may return to me. I am expecting him along with the brothers."*

and 2 Corinthians 8:16-18: *"I thank God, who put into the heart of Titus the same concern I have for you. For Titus not only welcomed our appeal, but he is coming to you with much enthusiasm and on his own initiative. And we are sending along with him the brother who is praised by all the churches for his service to the gospel."*

and 2 Corinthians 8:22-24: *"In addition, we are sending with them our brother who has often proved to us in many ways that he is zealous, and now even more so because of his great confidence in you. As for Titus, he is my partner and fellow worker among you; as for our brothers, they are representatives of the churches and an honor to Christ. Therefore, show these men the proof of your love and the reason for our pride in you, so that the churches can see it."*

Paul also expected the churches to support the wider Kingdom needs e.g. giving to the needs in another part of the world: 2 Corinthians 8 and 9 and Romans 15:25-27

Paul expected the Romans to receive him and support his ministry needs as he traveled to Spain: Romans 15:23-24: *"But now that there is no more place for me to work in these regions, and since I have been longing for many years to see you, I plan to do so when I go to Spain. I hope to visit you while passing through and to have you assist me on my journey there, after I have enjoyed your company for a while."*

Is this a one-way street in disguise? No – Paul poured into the churches wherever he went or wherever he sent a team member. He was called to encourage, equip and release people and he did it wherever he was. This is the foundation of accountability and oversight. Let us look at two examples (and there are many more):

The church in Thessalonica was planted during Paul's second missionary journey. Paul did not stay long as he was forced to flee because of persecution. Yet, they accepted the gospel and during the short time Paul and his companions built lasting relationships because of the way the lived and acted (see 1 Thessalonians 1:2-8). The apostolic team invested their lives in the church, e.g.:

> 1 Thessalonians 1:6-12: *"As apostles of Christ we could have been a burden to you, but we were gentle among you, <u>like a mother caring for her children</u>. We loved you so much that we were delighted to share with you not only the gospel of God, but our lives as well, because you had become so dear to us. Surely you remember, brothers, our toil and hardship; we worked night and day in order not to be a burden to anyone while we preached the gospel of God to you. You are witnesses and so is God, of how holy, righteous and blameless we were among you who believed. For you know that <u>we dealt with you as a father deals with his own children</u>, encouraging, comforting and urging you to live lives worthy of God, who calls you into his kingdom and glory."*

Paul and the apostolic teams with him invested their lives and built personal relationships with the churches and members. The concept of a father (or mother) is very central to grasp as we look at accountability and oversight. Paul dealt with major problems in the churches from time to time, but never "lorded" it over the people. He became a father in the faith, because of the way he led as servant! This is wonderfully illustrated in the way in which he responded to the many problems within the church in Corinth. In the chapter on apostleship he wrote in 1 Corinthians 4:14-17: *I am not writing this to shame you, but to warn you, as my dear children. <u>Even though you have ten thousand guardians in Christ, you do not have many fathers, for in Christ Jesus I became your father through the gospel</u>. Therefore, I urge you to imitate me. For this reason, I am sending to you Timothy, my son whom I love, who is faithful in the Lord. He will remind you of my way of life in Christ Jesus, which agrees with what I teach everywhere in every church."*

Oversight and accountability are rooted in relationship earned through servant leadership. Through Paul's service the local churches became strengthened and in return the strength of the local church opened the door for his ministry to become more effective, e.g.:

> 2 Corinthians 10:13-16: *"We, however, will not boast beyond proper limits, but will confine our boasting to the field God has assigned to us, a field that reaches even to you. We are not going too far in our boasting, as would be the case if we had not come to you, for we did get as far as you with the gospel of Christ. Neither do we go beyond our limits by boasting of work done by*

others. Our hope is that, as your faith continues to grow, our area of activity among you will greatly expand, so that we can preach the gospel in the regions beyond you. For we do not want to boast about work already done in another man's territory."

The fivefold ministry is to produce healthy local churches with a Kingdom mindset working with the apostolic leadership to build a supportive network that will cover an ever-increasing area for ministry. In practical terms, apostolic teams invest their resources to establish this type of a Kingdom network and they enter into covenant relationship with those who are willing to go the distance. They visit and send the leaders to home fellowships to build and strengthen the local church. They set up special times for the local leaders and members who commit to walk with them in full covenant relationship as we just described. They pull out all the stops and network local churches with others. In turn the local churches and leaders respond and go the extra mile and lay it all down for the bigger Kingdom vision.

It is all about the King and His Kingdom.

EPILOGUE

*A*s I wrote in the preface, this little booklet will challenge those who have a vested interest in the church structure, particularly those in leadership. It might even release fear in you. If that is the case, I simply ask that you take the challenge and with honesty seek the Lord's will. **However, this little booklet is first and foremost written for the many who are wandering around like sheep without a shepherd. It is written to those who have been disillusioned by the church and by the abuse that has originated in the structure of the organized church. It will also appeal to many in the church who are frustrated and who are used to fill slots and run ineffective programs, but who are not released in ministry.**

This little booklet is to share what God taught us since we started the journey of faith guided by a vision of a church as we read about in the New Testament. We dared to believe that it is possible to have that kind of church and church structure even in the modern Western world. We discovered that it is indeed true and in fact that we were not alone. On a small scale we have seen how this model can work. We are not alone. All over the world and even here in North America networks of home churches are being birthed and servant leadership practiced. Captives are set free. Many who are no-names in society move with confidence and power, as they are being equipped and released. The new wine is being poured out and in His grace our Lord has given us the guidelines for the new wineskin so that both the wine and wineskin will not be lost.

There is an incredible freedom as members minister to one another. Itinerant leaders visit home churches and equip and encourage many. They speak into lives as they earn the right through their servant leadership. Finances are handled with joy and liberality, particularly because the overhead is low without costly buildings, staff and program needs. Celebrations are joyful occasions where the networks are strengthened and divine appointments abound. In short, the model works.

How do we start? All you need is a home (or business) and someone else! Jesus said where two or three are gathered in His name, He will be there! Trust him! He will show up. We find that it is not difficult to begin. Just seek those who need a touch from God and invite them over. The Spirit has an amazing way to set up divine appointments and He works through His gifts in each of us. We see an incredible variety in the various churches reflecting the key gifts in the church. A leader with an evangelistic anointing will have many new believers in the church. Someone with a deliverance ministry will attract many who need deliverance and will rebuild broken lives. Personally, God has directed many with leadership abilities to us, as we understand the issues of control that stifle potential leaders in churches where there is a spirit of control.

It is important to walk in relationship with others and trust God to direct you to those with whom you should network. My personal observation: Whenever it looks like control, stay clear. Seek those who will walk with you in relationship and trust the Spirit to guide and direct. Each church is completely free to make its own decisions and to seek input or advice from others with whom they have relationship.

The church is free to network with any other church or individual. **If Jesus is the head of the church and His Spirit is all-powerful, I think they can handle the needs and keep the church on track!**

When Jesus outlined His ministry in the synagogue in Nazareth, He read from Isaiah 61. In John 20:21 the resurrected Lord said to His disciples:

"As the Father sent me, so I am sending you!"

This is the apostolic mandate of the church. We are sent in the same way as Jesus was sent

and to do the same as he did. That is why He gave us the Spirit and anointed us. With that, let us get our focus on the vision outlined in Isaiah 61:1-4: *"The Spirit of the Sovereign LORD is on me, because the LORD has anointed me to preach good news to the poor. He has sent me to bind up the brokenhearted, to proclaim freedom for the captives and release from darkness for the prisoners, to proclaim the year of the Lord's favor and the day of vengeance of our God, to comfort all who mourn and provide for those who grieve in Zion – to bestow on them a crown of beauty instead of ashes, the oil of gladness instead of mourning, and a garment of praise instead of a spirit of despair. They will be called oaks of righteousness, a planting of the LORD for the display of his splendor. <u>They will rebuild the ancient ruins and restore the places long devastated; they will renew the ruined cities that have been devastated for generations.</u>"*

Nearly two thousand years ago 11 disciples met the risen Lord while the doors were locked. They were hiding in fear. He appeared and then released the Holy Spirit to empower them. They left the security of the four walls and went into the world. These no-names went out in power and changed the world. They did not invest in buildings and programs. They did not care about titles and places of honor. They simply met in homes and wherever they could and shared their lives, which became part of the message. These are the foundations of the church and what we see today is a far cry from that. It is time for the no-names to move out of the captivity of the four walls of the church as many know it and simply be the church again. It is time for those wandering as sheep without a shepherd to pick up their ministry and be the church. **They will rebuild the ancient ruins and restore the places long devastated; they will renew the ruined cities that have been devastated for generations! Amen.**

ABOUT THE AUTHOR

*D*r. Willie Joubert was born in what was known as Tanganyika in East Africa and grew up on a farm that his parents pioneered after World War 2. It was an amazing childhood growing up in amidst wild animals with no hydro, phones, radios or TVs! When he was 11 they moved to a farm in South Africa. Going to school in the nearby town unbeknownst to him at the time was the fact that one of his classmates in Grade 6 would be his future wife.

Following graduation, he attended the University of Pretoria where he completed a Masters degree in Semitic Languages and a degree in Theology and subsequently a Ph.D. in Old Testament Studies. Dr. Joubert taught Semitic Languages for 7 years at the University of Pretoria before he immigrated to Canada with his wife, Eda, and three children. In Canada he pastored in traditional churches as Presbyterian Minister and then in non-denominational settings, worked in church planting as well as in prayer ministry and applying his faith in business settings and in support of para-church ministries. These journeys led to a re-examining of the Biblical foundations of the Church and a conclusion that the future of the church will necessitate a return to the simplicity of the early church in small home-based churches where ordinary people will do the work of ministry.

With this conviction Willie and Eda pioneered a home church and began to network with others. In the process he wrote a number of books and shared the copies with friends and with anyone interested in these. Recently he decided to formally publish them so that a wider audience can tap into the resources. This little book was the first in a series reflecting their journey of faith and form the foundation to grasp the concept of the Biblical foundations of the church. May it become a blessing to many!

Lightning Source UK Ltd.
Milton Keynes UK
UKHW021021210820
368606UK00016B/1168